Black Music in America

Black Music in America

JOHN RUBLOWSKY

CULTURE &
DISCOVERY

BASIC BOOKS, INC., PUBLISHERS

New York   London

© 1971 by Basic Books, Inc.
Library of Congress Catalog Card Number 71-135553
SBN 465–00697–3
Manufactured in the United States of America
Designed by Loretta Li

Contents

Illustrations

Black Music in America

1 A People's Music

A concert presented by the New York Philharmonic Society in November 1893 created a stir of excitement that affected nearly everyone in American music. It was the occasion of the world premiere of Anton Dvorak's Symphony No. 5, *From the New World*—the renowned Bohemian composer's new work that had been written in America.

Advance publicity had described the new symphony as a musical impression of the New World, and the music community was curious to hear how an established European composer would interpret America. But, although Dvorak's symphony has since become a favorite with concertgoers all over the world, its premiere was greeted with mixed feelings. It was by no means an immediate success.

To understand the reasons for this rather lukewarm reception, we must examine the state of American music at the time. Serious—or "art"—music in America was then dominated by a genteel tradition that ignored all native musical expression and looked for inspiration mainly to postromantic Germany. The music of the popular stage and that of the folk genre were dismissed from serious consideration as vulgar, cheap, and crude. In fact, as far as many in the music establishment were concerned, these forms did not exist. This opinion was reflected by Louis C. Elson, a leading musicologist of the time, who wrote in a respected music journal: "It must be admitted that in the field of folk music, America is rather barren."

A remarkable statement! Even more remarkable, this opinion was concurred in by most of his contemporaries. Thus Frederic L. Ritter, another respected musicologist, asked in his study of American music, published in 1883: "How are we to account for this *utter absence* of a national people's music and poetry in America?" (writer's emphasis).

To America's leading composers of the period, at least those who were recognized by the music establishment, music was an expression of the ideal; it existed on an ethereal plane, far removed from the everyday concerns of living. Actually, given the peculiar tenor of the time, this kind of attitude was inevitable. Since American popular and folk sources were ignored, "art" music could have no true roots, and without roots it had to retreat into an ivory tower. In a lecture given at Columbia University, Edward MacDowell, America's leading musical light of the time, said:

> The high mission of music is neither to be an agent for expressing material things, nor to utter pretty sounds to amuse the ear;

not a sensuous excitant to fire the blood, or a sedative to lull the senses; it is a language, but the language of the intangible, a soul language.

It would be difficult to argue with the high-sounding sentiments expressed by Professor MacDowell. He was undoubtedly sincere in his views. Yet, it was precisely this kind of misdirected idealism that cut serious music off from the mainstreams of American life. It helped create an intellectual atmosphere that made it possible for its advocates to ignore musical developments that were occurring everywhere in the New World—a posture which proved to be detrimental to music. Almost nothing from the great bulk of nineteenth-century American "art" music has survived the test of time. The "grand operas," "symphony concertantes," the "chorals" composed by a succession of learned and snobbish professors have for the most part, been forgotten.

Looking back now, one is at a loss to explain how such learned and influential scholars managed to overlook a music that was practically everywhere. Was it possible that they never heard a minstrel show or the sounds of a country barn-dance? Or was it simply that they were so wrapped up in an aesthetic and social mystique, they could not hear? Or was it, perhaps, a result of the racism that blights American history? Both American folk and popular music were, as we shall see, intimately connected with the musical life of the American Negro—a people who, at the time, had only recently been emancipated. Perhaps the scholars unconsciously recognized this derivation and refused to believe that anything of value could come from the despised blacks.

Dvorak, however, listened and found the land shaking with music. Unawed by the genteel tradition and comparatively untainted by American racism, he traveled about the country and sampled its varied offerings—the songs of black stevedores loading and unloading the steamboats that plied the Ohio and Mississippi rivers, the sprightly rhythms and sentimental poignancy of the minstrel show. Spirituals, in particular, fascinated him with their elegiac melodies and supple harmonies. As Henry Thacker Burleigh, a student of Dvorak's, described this appreciation years later:

> Dvorak was deeply impressed by the old Negro "spirituals." It was my privilege to sing repeatedly some of the old plantation songs for him at his home, and one in particular, "Swing Low, Sweet Chariot," greatly pleased him. . . . He used to stop and ask if that was the way the slaves sang.

Dvorak listened to and absorbed this music and utilized its spirit and genius in his compositions. It was this sensitivity to, and appreciation for, native American expression that was evident in the *New World* symphony and so unsettled American music circles. Here was a symphonic work, offered by a foreigner, that breathed the spirit of a music that was despised. To make matters worse, the composer made no secret of his sources. In a statement published in *The New York Times* before the premiere, Dvorak openly admitted that the spirit and themes of his new symphony were based upon native sources, especially the music of the Negro community.

> These beautiful and varied themes are the product of the soil. They are American. They are the folk music of America and your composers must turn to them. In the Negro melodies of America I discover all that is needed for the creation of a great and noble school of music.

Not so, answered our leading composers and musicologists. Typical was the reaction of Professor Edward MacDowell. In a scathing rebuttal to Dvorak, he summarily rejected the idea of an American music based upon the folklore of musically untutored blacks.

> We have here been offered a pattern for an American national musical costume by the Bohemian, Dvorak—though what Negro melodies have to do with Americanism in art still remains a mystery.... Masquerading in the so-called nationalism of Negro clothes cut in Bohemia cannot help American music.

It is odd that Anton Dvorak, the foreigner, the Bohemian, was able to recognize a "great and noble" music in the Negro melodies he heard in America while Edward MacDowell, American dreamer and high idealist, could hear nothing. Yet, this was a pattern that was to be repeated again and again in subsequent years when foreign musicians and composers were first to recognize the significance of American musical developments.

How do we account for this? The answer, in one important respect, is to be found in the long history of black music in America—a soft wind from Africa that was blown across the New World shores. And insofar as the history of this music is the history of a people, we must also look to the latter. What we find is one of the bleakest chapters in American history—a chapter that is too often ignored, glossed over, and distorted because it is so unpleasant. How do we confront the fact that throughout the first century of our history as a nation a sizable part of our population was enslaved? Slaves in a nation conceived in *liberty?* In a nation dedicated to the proposition that *all men are created equal?* There is a contradiction here that staggers the mind. How do we deal with such a fact? How do we explain it? The answer is that we do not. We sweep it under the rug and ignore it as best we can.

Most of us are at least familiar with the peoples and cultures of England, France, Germany, Spain, Italy, Russia. But how many of us, black or white, know anything at all about the Cormorantees, Sengalese, Yaruba, Benin, Dahomeans, Ibo, Bombara? Yet, all of these were West African peoples, each with a distinct language, history, and culture. These African peoples played an important role in American history, but their stories are not studied. It is as though these individual histories were erased in the "middle passage" that brought them from Africa to America. The diversity, the traditions, the languages of these African nationalities have been all but obliterated in our American ignorance.

Everyone tends to think the best of his own, and we Americans are no exception. We like to think of America as a land of freedom and justice, as a New World haven from the terror and tyranny of the old. We like to think of ourselves as a generous, peaceful, and kindly people and of our nation and its history as guided by high moral purposes. We do not enjoy being reminded that not all of our history was noble, that greed, hypocrisy, and cruelty are also entwined in our history like so many scarlet threads. So, we tend to ignore those aspects and hope that they will be forgotten.

The opening of the Americas fired the imagination of people all over Europe, but from the very first acts of colonization, the American experience became polarized into two never-to-be-reconciled extremes. On the one hand, the New World evoked the highest idealism and noblest aspirations in the peoples of Europe. On the other, it stimulated greed and dreams of avarice.

In one sense, America was Europe's second chance—a divinely provided opportunity to create a new and more human society, free of the entrenched evils of the old. It offered a promise for fulfillment of the age-old dream of a golden land with liberty and justice for all. There, across the ocean, was a New World, rich beyond imagining, with land and room for all. This attitude was reflected in a poem written in London near the end of the eighteenth century by the English mystic William Blake.

> Though born on the cheating banks of Thames,
> Though his waters bathed my infant limbs,
> The Ohio shall wash his stains from me:
> I was born a slave, but I go to be free.

But America had become an extension of the total European consciousness, and all of the sins and evils of the Old World, along with the idealism, were projected into the New. We see this nether side exposed in the papers of a London merchant-financier, a contemporary of Blake. The document in question, addressed to the manager of a Jamaica sugar plantation, advised that a careful analysis of the figures compiled in the London countinghouse indicated that economy could best be served by working a slave to death in seven years. Appropriate suggestions for accomplishing this ideal of efficient management were forwarded to the manager who, we have no reason to doubt, applied them conscientiously.

It is obvious that the situation of the black man in the New World bore no comparison to that of the others who came to these shores. Unlike the great bulk of the white population, he came neither to search for freedom nor to fulfill dreams of avarice. He came forcibly, as a slave, as another man's property. He came in chains, uprooted from his culture and tradition. In the passage to the New World, African families were separated, fellow nationals were carefully segregated, friends were taken from each other. The African thereby came to America stripped of his past, for the past is more than memory. It is shared experience, a mutual tradition and history, a common language.

The slave master, by necessity a shrewd, practical psychologist, knew the importance of cultural destruction in the creation of obedient, docile slaves. Culture makes a man bigger than his individual self; it joins him into a larger, stronger whole. Take away this culture and you take away a large part of the man. What is left is the raw human energy upon which all the formative powers of the whip and chain can be exercised.

Thus transported to a hostile new world under the worst possible circumstances, the African was compelled to create a new tradition, a new myth in place of his obliterated past. And in the construction of this new tradition, the creativity of the African centered primarily upon music—music was his solace and release. In truth, he had no other choice, since other forms of creativity were denied him.

The visual arts, for example, were out of reach despite an African tradition of painting, sculpture, and design that rivaled that of any other culture. Indeed, this art exerted a profound influence upon European (and American) art when it became available in the nineteenth century. But for the slave, the visual arts were beyond aspiration. It takes a certain amount of leisure to develop the necessary skills and wealth to procure tools and materials. Neither was available to the slave. Similar limitations prevented the development of a literature. It was against the law—a crime—to permit a slave to learn how to read and write, and without these basic skills, it becomes almost impossible to create a literature.[1]

Also denied him was the art inherent in the history and mythology of America, though for a different reason. History is art to the extent that it is modified by the chauvinism and "wish-factor" of a particular population. The history of America as taught in our schools is different from that taught in England. In English history, George Washington was a rebel and a traitor.

To the slave, moreover, America's heroes, her patriotic slogans, and her endless talk of liberty and freedom held no magic. The constitution stated that "all men are created equal." Was the slave, then, not a man? It is not surprising, therefore, that the slave's attitude toward the myths and traditions of American history was different from that of the master. The view of one black poet, the late Langston Hughes, is exemplary.

> Let's make America America again
> Not that it ever was.

Thus music was the only artistic channel through which the slave could express the longings of his soul, the one outlet into which his creative energies could be funneled.

Basically, music demands no more than the human body for expression—a voice to sing out the melody, hands and feet to beat the rhythm. Instruments and leisure are superfluous. One can sing while working; indeed, hard work is made easier by singing. And hard work was the lot of the slave in America.

---

[1]The blacks did, however, develop a rich oral poetry which is only now beginning to be appreciated. As a pithy "slang" idiom this poetry has become part of our American verbal expression.

The slave became a kind of New World cultural catalyst, combining the various musical strains that had been brought into the Americas into a new and unique musical expression. So influential has this creativity been, that today it pervades all of American music. Delve deeply into almost any aspect of this music and you will eventually come upon a source in the African experience.

For years it was argued that this music was strictly a New World phenomenon. The assumptions behind this argument were the widely held beliefs that Africa had no culture to speak of and that what little of an African tradition was retained by the Africans when they reached the new world was soon overpowered by the "superior" white cultures. Modern research and scholarship, however, refute both of these assumptions and support the contention that Africa, during the period of the slave trade, had rich, proud cultures whose traditions continued to influence the transplanted black population. Studies by musicologists have revealed, for example, that the musical forms and styles of West Africa (the region from which most of the slaves came) are embedded in the music of black America to this day. They are present in the call-and-response pattern of the work song and "field holler"; in the supple harmonies of the "spiritual"; and in the vitality of "gospel" singing. All of American popular music, from the "minstrel tunes" of the nineteenth century to the "rock and roll" explosion of today, owes a debt to that indefinable musical quality that came to America from Africa—that quality we call "Soul!"

2 Africa

On a recent television "special," John Glenn, the astronaut, was featured in a program that retraced the steps of Henry Morton Stanley, adventurer, explorer, and newspaper reporter, in his historic quest for Dr. Livingston in the heart of unexplored Africa—unexplored, that is, by white men. Africans, of course, had lived there for millennia and had thoroughly explored their homeland. Still, it seemed like a good idea for a TV program—John Glenn, first American into space, presenting Stanley, who "opened" the mysterious reaches of "darkest" Africa.

The program began with standard African jungle footage, as a narrator spoke words to the effect that it was less than 100 years ago that the English first brought *light* into the heart of Africa. LIGHT? A more accurate description of this historical event would have inspired a different choice of words. Robbery, plunder, exploitation, murder, destruction, and humiliation would have been more appropriate metaphors. LIGHT? Hardly!

Yet, no great outcry was heard in protest of this historical distortion. The inaccuracy of the statement might, perhaps, have been noted by a specialist here and there but it was accepted readily, for the most part, because it fit into the myth which has come to surround Africa and Africans—a myth, some 400 years in the making, compounded of deliberate distortion and ignorance.

What do you think of when you hear the word "Africa"? If you are like most of us, a mixed picture comes to mind, made up of snatches from old Tarzan movies and jungle safari thrillers. We see brave white hunters moving through "savage-infested" jungles, as lions and elephants scatter before them through the impenetrable underbrush. "Good" natives faithfully carry the whiteman's burdens—balanced on their heads, generally—while "bad" natives lurk in the bushes with painted faces and long spears, preparing cowardly ambushes of the white hunter's party to the accompaniment of throbbing drums.

These are, of course, the simplest myths, but they are, perhaps, the most pervasive. Lions, for example, do not live in jungles but in semi-arid grasslands. Moreover, contrary to belief, only about 5 percent of the continent can be classified as jungle. But since jungles go with darkness and wild beasts, the lions will probably prowl through them forever—if only in our imaginations.

The myth of Africa as the "dark" continent is equally persistent. In this view, the Africa that predated European "enlightenment" is conceived of as a great land mass completely isolated from the rest of the world and festering in its own barbarity and backwardness. Actually, for the greater part of history, it was Europe that was isolated—more isolated than Africa ever was. During the Middle Ages, for example, while Europe was bogged down in a quagmire of small, warring dukedoms and principalities, Africans, Arabs, and Indians maintained an active trade across the Indian Ocean, the Sahara, and, on a small scale, across the Mediterranean.

Thus ivory and Morocco leather, products from south of the Sahara desert, were secured by Europeans from North Africans. Similarly, when, during the twelfth and thirteenth centuries, cowrie shells became a kind of currency throughout the African subcontinent south of the Sahara, they were brought from the Maldive Islands via Venice and the Arabs. Africa was even in touch with the fringes of Europe, as evidenced by portraits of Africans on Greek vases and portrait busts of blacks in Roman art. Historically, it was Europe, not Africa, that finally woke up after the fifteenth century.

Probably the most persistent and damaging myth is the one that sees Africa as "savage." This myth is a comparatively recent invention, having come into existence only in the eighteenth and nineteenth centuries, when "savages" became a philosophical necessity for the explosive emergence of European domination. The chronology of this concept is dramatically illustrated by a comparison of Shakespeare's treatment of an African in *Othello*, written at the beginning of the seventeenth century (1601), with Joseph Conrad's treatment in *Heart of Darkness*, written at the end of the nineteenth century.

Shakespeare's Othello was a fully conceived human being

of almost heroic proportions, with all of the passions, ambitions, and desires of the human attribute. The fact that he was black was incidental to the conception of his character; it was merely an additional dramatic device. In the Conrad story, however, the Africans are shadowy beings, without form or substance—little more than projections of the white man's guilt and fears. Some 300 years separate these two writers, a span of time during which not only the wealth of Africa was plundered but the humanity of Africans was despoiled as well.

Although the myth of African savagery was used as a rationale for the heartless exploitation of black people by calculating business interests, European missionaries were probably the most important factor in creating and maintaining this myth. It is an all too human tendency to exaggerate one's accomplishments, and the missionary was no exception. The more savage the people, the greater was the missionary's task. Moreover, the undeniable fortitude in the face of real hardships that some missionaries bore was very readily translated into a conquest of savagery by congregations and mission societies at home. Though many missionaries, as their writings show, were levelheaded observers who did not themselves exaggerate their conditions, it was this unfortunate image of heroes doing battle with cannibalism, lust and depravity—the traditional forces of "darkness"—that predominated.

Hopefully, today, we can admit the facts upon which such myths were based, and be objective about them. African culture, far from being alien to the European, shares more of its traits, its history, its social organization with Europe than does Asia and certainly more than does the American aborigine.

In the economic sphere, particularly with regard to agricultural methods, Africa and Europe were united by a similar approach. Indeed, the American plantation system, utilized in the production of sugar and cotton, was modeled after West African patterns. Marketing organization was also almost identical, so much so that an Italian or French peasant would have felt very much at home in a Sengalese or Dahomean market. And craftsmen in African societies were organized into guilds very much like those in Europe during the Middle Ages. There were guilds of weavers, ironworkers, musicians, sculptors, boatbuilders, and carvers, which not only passed on skills and traditions to apprentices but also dominated the practice of the various trade skills. Again, a European weaver or ironworker would have been right at home in the African organization.

African religions, as another example, are recognized today as variations on the same basic themes that dominate European religions. Both are fundamentally agricultural religious systems, which celebrate the cycle of the year and the harvest. In African religions there is the equivalent of Easter and Passover celebrations to mark the annual rebirth of the earth and the year; there are also equivalents of Christmas and Thanksgiving celebrations to mark the winter solstice and harvest periods.

In one respect, at least, the African religions reveal a higher moral sense than the European. In the African view, all of nature is imbued with sanctity—trees, rivers, mountains, animals, all contain a "spirit"—and with sanctity comes respect. When an African chopped down a tree, for example, or slew an antelope, he did so only after ceremonially propitiating its spirit, and even then he probably felt a twinge of remorse at the act. The Christian had no such compunctions, for in the

Judaeo-Christian tradition, nature is man's to dominate and exploit. The effects of this moral blindness are now being felt throughout the world in the critical despoliation of the environment, which threatens the very existence of man.

Family organization in West African society can also be linked to that of Europe through common values and forms. Even language is related structurally and grammatically, so that it is much easier for a European to learn to speak the Ibo tongue than Chinese or Japanese.

Finally, unlike some of the peoples of the Pacific and the Americas, Africans, both in Africa and abroad, have shown little resistance to change or so-called modernization. This factor, again, may stem largely from the fundamental similarity of African and European (including American) cultures. Historical evidence indicates a common pool of culture shared in the ancient past. Although the African manifestations are different, in many respects, from those of Europeans, the differences are superficial when compared to the gulfs that separate either from the Japanese, Malayans, or American Indians. Perhaps even more significant is the fact that Africa must have also shared Europe's pool of diseases since Africans were not decimated upon contact with the Europeans.

However, nowhere is this sharing of a common pool of culture more obvious than in music. At a very basic level, African musical expression is closely related to the European. The utilization of the voice and instruments is almost the same, and on a more fundamental level, the diatonic scale (the octave divided into seven steps) is common to both musical systems. This last forms the strongest link between them and is, as well, the mark that distinguishes them from all other systems. There is also a shared concept of harmony and a similar metronomic rhythmic concept. Altogether, these factors make African music intelligible to the European ear and vice versa.

Song was, and is, the characteristic musical expression of Africa. The African expressed all his feelings in song. Thus, there were songs for every occasion—for marriages and funerals, for ceremonies and festivals, for love and war, work and worship. The African taunted his enemies or rivals with songs of derision, he propitiated or implored his deities with an endless number of sacred melodies; he sang while he worked.

Parallel to song in African cultural expression, and occupying a position of equal prominence was the dance. Song and dance were inseparable, so much so that it would have been impossible to think of one without the other. There were sacred dances performed for religious rites; dances to prepare soldiers for war; wedding dances and funeral dances; harvest dances and planting dances; comic dances and solemn dances. Richard A. Waterman, in his study of *African Influences on the Music of the Americas,* described the musical consequences of this African preoccupation with dance.

> Essentially ... African music, with few exceptions, is to be regarded as music for the dance, although the "dance" involved may be entirely a mental one. Since this metronomic sense is of such basic importance, it is obvious that the music is conceived and executed in terms of it; it is assumed without question or consideration to be part of the conceptual equipment of both musicians and listeners and is, in the most complete way, taken for granted. When the beat is actually sounded, it serves as a confirmation of this subjective beat.

West African music was already highly developed and evolved when Portuguese navigators first made contact with the civilizations that existed along the Atlantic coast of Africa, or the Gold Coast. Almost all of these societies supported a sizable number of professional musicians, who were organized into guilds, along with such other artisans and craftsmen as wood carvers, weavers, and bronze casters. A professional musical caste meant that music was considered important enough by the society to allow its musicians the leisure and the opportunity to develop their art.

Like most guilds, the musical guilds were primarily family organizations; that is, it was more likely that the children of musicians would follow in the profession than the children of nonmusicians. The musical guilds in West Africa, however, were by no means closed, and anyone with the inclination and talent could be a candidate for membership.

Training for the would-be musician was arduous and involved. The aspirant generally entered the guild as a child and served a long apprenticeship before being admitted to full membership. This was no easy task, for the West African musician had to be master of a number of instruments that included a variety of wind instruments, both plucked and bowed string instruments, different kinds of xylophones, and a huge choice of drums, each with a peculiar timbre and percussive character.

The early Portuguese and later Dutch and Swedish travelers to West Africa in the mid-fifteenth century brought back tales of great kingdoms and cities along the coast. The capitol city of Benin, for example, was described as being more than ten miles across, surrounded by a moat and walls ten feet high. The palace itself was huge and elaborate, with dozens of apartments and galleries, large parade grounds, and exquisite gardens. Everywhere one looked there were magnificent carvings in ivory and wood, and castings in brass, bronze, gold, and silver. All of the actions of the king were surrounded with a pomp and ceremony that rivaled anything in Europe.

Yet, Benin was only one of the kingdoms of West Africa during this period. Literally hundreds of such kingdoms and principalities had developed along the Atlantic coast. Most had distinct languages and cultural traditions, so that people living within hailing distance could not, in many instances, speak each other's language. Within this diversity, however, there was great similarity. Most of the West African kingdoms were based upon agriculture and depended upon highly organized farming and stock raising for their wealth. The king, in most cases, was a sacred, Pharaoh-like figure, all of whose actions were circumscribed by elaborate rites and ceremony.

Slavery, too, was an element in all of these kingdoms, but slavery of a different kind than that which developed in the Western Hemisphere. For one thing, it was a benign slavery. To understand this difference, we must examine the tradition of slavery as it existed in Europe and Africa at the time. African slavery was primarily a state institution, with only few exceptions. The slave was basically a "kin-less" person who was attached to a household or family group by "non-kinship" links, often of a servile nature. Such slaves did work, often the hardest and lowliest, but they married, brought their families into the social group, had prescribed rights and privileges, and could even enter the church or the professional guilds.

European slavery, on the other hand, was primarily economic and had no overtones of kinship or family. The slave was nothing more than a work unit. This tradition was ancient and firmly established. Even in Aristotle's time slaves were worked to death in the salt mines—thence, the well-known expression. It did not originate in Africa.

The histories of these West African kingdoms are obscure. The entire area has been neglected by archaeological and scientific study. Whatever clues we have to West Africa's distant past have surfaced, for the most part, by accident. Strange stone figurines, for example, resembling nothing previously unearthed, have been turned up in an area stretching from Lake Chad all the way to the Guinea coast. Badly weathered, they appear to be very old. Where do they come from? Who made them? We cannot be sure.

Probably the most important of these chance archeological finds occurred near Jos, Nigeria. Tin miners in search of ore uncovered the remains of an old and particularly long-lived settlement—now called the Nok culture—which flourished between 1000 B.C. and 200 A.D. The knowledge of the Nok people as farmers and artists has been pieced together from the debris—from the stone tools found in the earliest layers, from the iron tools, the grains of millet, and the beautiful little heads of fired clay found throughout the site. The latter suggest even more. They suggest a long artistic tradition and a society with enough means, enough leisure and wealth to allow such a tradition to develop.

This tradition has been traced beyond the Nok culture itself. It apparently moved along with migratory groups and tribes as they wandered south, away from the savannah lands and down toward the great forest fringe along the Guinea coast. A thousand years after the last Nok head had been modeled, city artists in southern Nigeria created remarkable likenesses of their kings in clay and terra cotta. Their work is glorious by any standard, rivaling the best sculptures of Egypt or Greece. Still later, the same artistic

Early eighteenth-century bronze casting from Benin reflects an ancient West African artistic tradition. The skillful castings presuppose a high level of technological development among the artists who made them. (*The Bettmann Archive*)

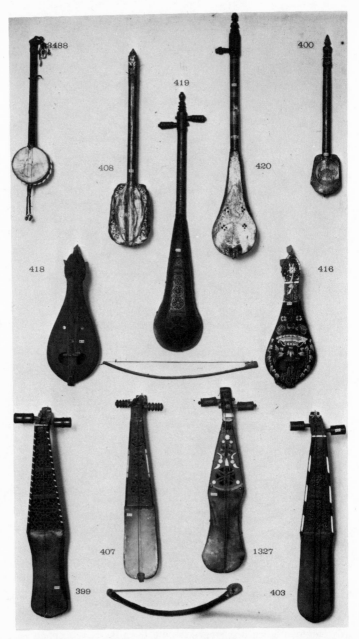

Early nineteenth-century West African stringed instruments, including both plucked and bowed instruments, demonstrate a high level of craftsmanship and a sophisticated knowledge of sound production. (*Metropolitan Museum of Art, The Crosby Brown Collection, 1899*)

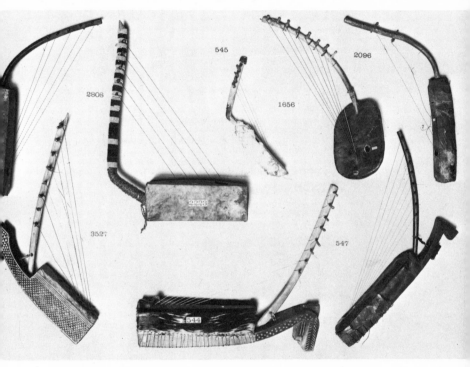

West African harps show the range and skill of the craftsmen who made them. (*Metropolitan Museum of Art, The Crosby Brown Collection, 1899*)

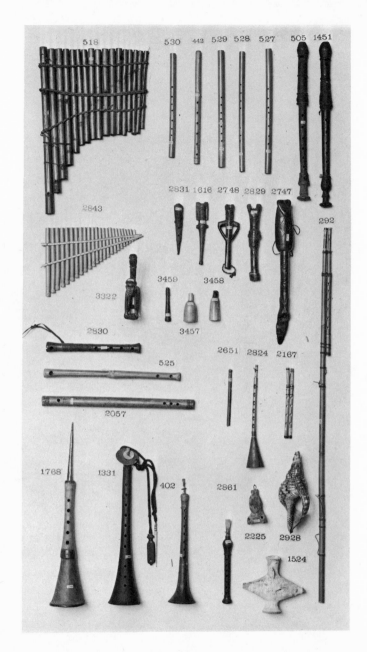

A variety of West African flutes, conch-shell horns, and tempered pipes attest the high development of wind instruments in African music. (*Metropolitan Museum of Art, The Crosby Brown Collection, 1899*)

A sampling of West African drums. Nowhere else in the world has there been so detailed and varied a development of percussive instruments. *(Metropolitan Museum of Art, The Crosby Brown Collection, 1899)*

The communication drum is still used in outlying areas of the Congo. This method of communication utilizes the patterns and rhythms of speech rather than a set code to transmit messages. *(United Press Photo)*

tradition was expressed in bronze and brass, silver and gold, with the same elegance and grace. Indeed, the Benin and Dahomean bronze castings, made with the lost-wax process, are considered among the finest made anywhere in the world.

On the West African coast between modern Ghana and Nigeria there is a natural break in the rain forest. In that wedge of clear, gently rolling land lies Dahomey, which was, until French conquest in 1892, a powerful kingdom—perhaps the most powerful in its part of the world. In many ways, Dahomey was typical of the West African kingdoms, and its historical record is more complete than most.

News of Dahomey and its treasures reached Europe by the seventeenth century. A hundred years later the kingdom was famous among sea traders. Many travelers and writers have, at one time or another, visited Dahomey and written about the nation and its society. Among them was the British explorer Sir Richard Burton, who undertook a diplomatic mission to King Gelele in 1864 and described the kingdom in his journals. In 1931 Melville Herskovits, the American anthropologist, and his wife came to study. Though the monarchy was then forty years in the past, they found Dahomey much as Burton had described it almost one hundred years earlier.

Just when and where the first king of Dahomey got his start is uncertain. The Dahomey or Fon people migrated toward the sea from an area around the headwaters of the Niger river sometime near the beginning of the seventeenth century. By 1625, their war bands had conquered Abomey, about 90 miles from the coast, which became the capital. In village after village, conquest was effected with little struggle; the local chief or king did homage to the invading monarch and joined the Dahomean kingdom.

The organization of the Dahomean society was founded upon three basic factors: a legal system, which bound the people in a rule of law; a system of cooperative guilds, which regulated the economic life of the society; and an elaborate, accurate, and continuous census, which monitored the population. The result was a society that was backward in some respects (there was no written language, for example) and very advanced in others (the social status of Dahomean women is only being reached now in the countries of Europe and America). In most respects, however, Dahomean society was admirably adapted to the peculiar physical and spiritual conditions of its people. Most visitors to Dahomey noted the cheerful good nature of its inhabitants, the formalized etiquette and manners, the intelligence and industriousness of the people.

The legal system was organized around a graduated series of courts administered by a guild of professional lawyers, or advocates, and with judges appointed by the king. Each step in the judicial system—from the local, to the provincial, to the king, himself, who represented the final court of appeal for all Dahomeans—was proscribed by inviolate rules and laws and appropriate rites and ceremony.

Local courts could hear only minor disputes and could deliver only limited rulings—no more than four days in jail or a small fine. Offenses or disagreements requiring more extensive punishment had to be heard in the provincial cities. The prospect of high court costs, however, was usually enough to induce quarreling villagers to accept quick settlements at home.

Final appeals went directly to the king, as did all cases for which capital punishment or enslavement might be the result.

"Death is mine," the Dahomean monarch decreed in effect. This rule applied to all, noble or commoner, slave or freeman. To enforce this rule, the equivalent of a coroner's jury investigated every death in the kingdom for evidence of foul play.

The cooperative guild system, which dominated the economic life of Dahomey, had, for as long as anyone could remember, been part of the land. These guilds, generally organized on family lines, were, in a manner of speaking, the original owners of the land. Before the Dahomean kings had come, they were there, and remnants of the system can still be perceived in modern Dahomey. They symbolized something more than work and land; they were an embodiment of the spirit of cooperation that was central to Dahomean life.

Not only were these self-help clubs instrumental in the raising of food and the building of homes, but one could, in such a group, beat the high cost of buying, marrying, or dying. Smiths and weavers, for example, pooled funds for raw materials, and potters did their firing together in a common oven. When it came to weddings and funerals— always occasions for ostentatious display in Dahomey—only mutual "insurance" saved the family from bankruptcy.

As symbols of this ancient cooperative spirit, the work or guild leaders were potential rivals to the power of the king. Worse yet, they were all but untouchable. Their age-old connections with the land and the spirits of the land kept them out of royal reach. The Dahomean kings, however, were practical politicians if nothing else. What they could not beat, they joined. Village chiefs were ignored, but village guild leaders were praised, pampered, and honored.

When a new man attained the power of guild leader he was given his day in court. He came to Abomey where, amid

all the pomp and ceremony of the royal palace, he was presented to the king and received, in the presence of all the
important dignitaries of the kingdom, a badge of office and
many gifts. It must have been rather like achieving knight-
hood in England. After returning to his village, the guild
leader was bound to the king by these ceremonial rites, as
much as by law or royal power.

One of the most important aspects of Dahomean administration was the census. Everyone had to pay taxes; everyone
—men and women—had to do military duty; and everyone
had to fulfill certain royal work obligations. In order to
administer these duties the king had to know the number
and whereabouts of his subjects, and he accomplished this
by means of a continuous census.

The Dahomeans may not have known how to read or
write, but they certainly could count. Every eight days the
king received news of all births and deaths in the area
around Abomey, the capital city, and every three months he
received reports from the provincial capitals. He was told
whether the deceased were children or adults, their age,
sex, social status, and the manner of death. Pebbles in special
sacks gave the numbers, pictures on the sacks told the village,
and colors and various emblems supplied additional information.

The count of children was kept in two sets of boxes—one
for boys, the other for girls—with 13 boxes to a set. Pebbles
were placed in the first boxes as births were reported and
removed as deaths occurred; then, as the year passed, all were
transferred to the next higher box. After their thirteenth
year, children assumed the status of adults, and their pebbles
were sent along to fill adult sacks corresponding to their
localities.

These population records were kept in a long, low building with many doors and many rooms, each representing a city or province, and a king's reign that was located in a central area within the royal enclave. When a new king gained the throne, he was taken to the house of the census as his first official act. Priests guided him from room to room, showing him Dahomeans in their numbers, reign by reign. "Make the people grow," he was told. "Protect them, nourish them, make them great."

After this initial visit, the matter of population became both secret and sacred information. Only two persons shared this knowledge with the king: the chief census taker and one of the king's female advisers, who were called "mothers." These special "mothers" of Dahomey were, in reality, wives of the king, and there were thousands of them. They were the nation's recorders and filing system, its supervisors, and, as the eyes and ears of the king, they were also the country's secret service.

Each official in the government had his assigned "mother" —a watchful lady who accompanied him to every meeting, sat in on every conference and commercial transaction. Whatever he reported to the king, she was called upon to verify. If she did not, the official was in trouble. The king was kept informed by a constant stream of reports that arrived at the palace from every corner of Dahomey. Since there was no written language, the messages had to be memorized. Two messengers were usually assigned to each message, to make certain that the information was accurate. The specially trimmed hair and royal staffs of the messengers, former war heroes, proclaimed their office. Running in relays, day and night, these messengers could cover the 90 miles between Abomey and the coast in less than two days.

Even the army had its "mothers." Each male soldier, whether private or general, had his female counterpart. Because some of the kings preferred the women warriors, they tended to favor them and heap them with praise and rewards. Actually, the women fought as hard as the men and, it was said, were even fiercer and more ruthless in battle. The existence of a large army of women—all of whom were theoretically married to the king—resulted in a nation full of fierce old maids, who commanded considerable political power, and a very slow growth of population.

Religion in Dahomey was not monolithic. There were a number of great temples that represented competing denominations. Most prominent were those that served the principal deities of earth, sky, and thunder. There were also smaller groups which honored less impressive, but more personal gods. A universal favorite was the messenger of the gods, a cosmic cutup who might be induced to change the orders from on high, bringing a fate other than that which had been ordained down to earth.

Temples were served by devotees to whom varying degrees of sanctity were ascribed. The hierarchy was somewhat analogous to that of lay brother, preaching brother, and priest. Training for any of these offices was difficult and involved. Even that of a lay brother required a novitiate of nearly a year and carried no guarantee of appointment. However, exacting though the priesthood was, it was not exclusive. Everyone, slaves and women included, was welcome to undertake the novitiate; even the opportunity to rise in the hierarchy was extended to all. There were, in fact, always more women novices than men—a fact that grumbling husbands attributed to the women's desire for the fancy costumes and the chance to take on airs at home.

Dahomean men, in reality, had a lot to grumble about as far as the women were concerned. Compared to most other societies—including our own—their women enjoyed a remarkably liberated status, barred only from certain official offices and the trade guilds. Women voted—a right won in America only in 1920—and served as priests, novitiates, and fighting soldiers. They could, moreover, earn, keep, and inherit money and property; women in the West, in contrast, only acquired this right legally about 70 years ago. Very often, in fact, Dahomean women had more money than men and could provide for their children's weddings and even, if they were so inclined, help their husbands acquire an extra wife or two. They earned their money, not in the fields or in the crafts, but in the market place.

Women were the merchants and entrepreneurs of Dahomey. They managed whatever there was of high finance—remitting to the king his share of the take, of course. So firmly established was commerce as a female calling that little girls played at buying and selling much as little girls in America play with dolls. A new baby was not fully recognized or named until his mother had introduced him into the market.

The status of women was, furthermore, reflected in the marriage institution. It was almost impossible, for example, for a man to get a divorce; it was considered both ungallant for him to do so and magically unsafe. Divorce was the woman's prerogative, and she could dissolve a marriage almost at will. As to marriage, itself, there was ample room for choice as far as the bride was concerned. Our conventional ceremonies offer a couple only two options with regard to nuptial vows. The bride can promise to "love, honor and obey" or to "love, honor and cherish." That is all. In Dahomey there were thirteen sets of vows, covering all sorts of marriage arrangements. There was even a provision for "woman" marriage, in which a lady of great wealth or noble birth could create and head her own family. She did this by "marrying" slave girls or commoners and then lending them to her own brothers, cousins, or male friends. Whatever children resulted then called the wealthy woman "father," took her name, and inherited her wealth.

Great though it was, the freedom granted the woman in Dahomey bore no comparison to that enjoyed by the artist— he could defy the king. Certain crafts such as gold and silver smithing and the weaving of cloth for ceremonial clothes were confined to the members of tight family guilds, forever under the king's thumb. But sculpture and music were arts that were open to anyone with talent and free spirit. Both arts were popular, and almost all Dahomeans tried their hands at them. The professional musician and sculptor, however, had to belong to a guild and undergo a long period of training and apprenticeship.

The wood carvers of Dahomey, in particular, had a reputation for temperament. Women considered them dubious marriage prospects, though they were sought after by women with enough wealth to keep them in style. Dreamy and unreliable, they were forever wandering around the forests looking for suitable wood when they should have been at home working. They never finished commissions on time, and what is worse, they never seemed to care. The king, himself, was known to plead with artists and even, on occasion, to have them put under lock and key until their work was done. However, never did he push the artist too hard or threaten too seriously. Good artists, after all, did not grow on trees.

If the sculptors of Dahomey were temperamental, the musicians were the playboys of the Dahomean world. They

were the pampered darlings of society and enjoyed a pecu-
liarly privileged status. This is not very surprising when we
recall the importance of music in the Dahomean world. Music
was everywhere—part of religious ritual, secular festivities,
all ceremonies, even work. The Dahomean musician was thus
in constant demand, his talents called upon for almost every
important occasion from birth to death.

Since anyone could become an artist or a musician, these
professions tended to become very competitive and demand-
ing, and the professional had to be good. The Dahomean boy
who decided upon a career in music, for example, entered
upon a long and arduous period of training. In order to gain
entry into the guild, he had to be a combination instrumentalist, singer, composer, dancing master, and poet. He had to
be able to lead a congregation through the intricate steps of
elaborate dances, both sacred and secular, as well as demonstrate an ability to improvise songs spontaneously on any
given subject.

It was from this land of Dahomey that a steady stream of
emigrants came to America over a period of some 250 years.
They came, of course, as slaves packed into the holds of the
"big black birds"—the slave ships, America bound. The
Dahomean kings, along with all the other rulers up and down
the coast, earned a good part of their wealth by supplying
this demand. They supplied it, in the main, with captives
taken in war, with convicted criminals and debtors, and
political prisoners. It was a convenient way to dispose of
political rivals.

Enslavement was a harsh fate. Many Dahomeans con-
signed to slavery did not survive the passage overseas. Many
who did survive must have often wished for death. Yet,
despite the misery, despite the hardships, they brought some-

thing of Dahomey with them, something that has worked its way into the fabric of American life. They brought their gods, for one thing, and the concept of the spirit of god in all. They brought their mysticism and spiritual passion. They brought their manner of worship—the use of song and dance, the clapping of hands, and the antiphonal response. They brought their talent for organization and used it, again and again, in bloody revolts. They brought their elaborate sense of etiquette, their formalized good manners, and ceremonial address. They brought the tradition of strong-minded, independent, and resourceful women. They brought the spirit of cooperation and the capacity for optimism and good cheer that characterized them in their homelands and marks their descendants to this day. They brought their musical feelings and artistic talents. And finally, they brought their capacity to survive in the face of incredible hardships and abuse.

ろ The Slave Trade

Oddly enough, slavery was a product of civilization. It was unknown as an institution among earlier peoples, who sustained themselves on a day-to-day basis by hunting, fishing, and other survival-oriented activities. The discovery of agriculture and the development of herding and animal husbandry changed the nomadic life of the hunter into the more settled life of the farmer, the villager, and ultimately the citydweller. The ability to produce surplus agricultural and industrial products under these conditions made human slavery profitable—for the slave owner, that is, not for the slave.

In its initial stages, slavery was not associated with a particular race or people; the slave was invariably a "foreigner" captured in war and forced to work for his captors. In one sense, slavery may be regarded as a preferable substitute for the more primitive practice of killing captives. Will Durant has remarked upon this aspect of slavery. "It was a great moral improvement when men ceased to kill or eat their fellow men and merely made them slaves." But, as civilization developed and the power of the ruling classes was strengthened and institutionalized, slavery was gradually extended to people who were not "foreign." Defaulting debtors, criminals, children abandoned by their parents, poor people in general who were without influence, and political rivals to those in power were enslaved. Finally, in the more advanced societies, the practice of conducting raids upon neighbors for the purpose of capturing slaves became widespread. In time, these societies—which included the Roman, and certain African, kingdoms—became increasingly warlike and aggressive in order to maintain and enlarge the supply of slaves. The expropriated labor of these slaves, in turn, added to the material and martial strength of the society.

To a great extent, these changes were merely reflections of changes in the philosophy of slave ownership. In its earliest forms, slavery was seen as a method for appropriating the products of labor, above the minimum necessary to keep the laborer alive, to those who held control over the slave. In a later stage, slave ownership, per se, became a principal attribute of power, and most slaves were possessed by the state or by the ruling class that monopolized the power of the state. Then, as small city-states embarked upon empire building and extensive warfare, the number of slaves increased and institutions and practices associated with slavery grew more complex. The height of exploitation of the slave's labor was reached with the advent of individual ownership of slaves.

As an institutionalized form of robbery, slavery provided a means for the accumulation of wealth, which was impossible in the earlier, food-gathering stage of human history. It thus created the means by which a leisure class could be sustained, and this leisure, in turn, encouraged the intellectual and material achievements of these slave-based civilizations. Some historians maintain that slavery gave man traditions and habits of toil, possibly the beginnings of a work ethic, which later contributed to the industrial growth of modern times. But, if slavery accomplished these things, the cost was high in terms of the brutalization, hatred, and degradation the institution unleashed.

When the Portuguese first made contact with West Africa at the beginning of the fifteenth century, they found a number of well-established kingdoms along the Guinea coast and at the mouth of the Congo River. Here were great cities with elaborate palaces and regal courts administered with appropriate pomp and ceremony. Slavery was an element in all of these civilizations, but it was essentially an institution of the state and the kings; that is, most of the slaves were bound either to the king or the state. Furthermore, the number was not very great and protection was provided in the law and tradition.

The Portuguese established trading relations with these kingdoms, and one of the first items in this commerce was slaves. The African kings saw nothing wrong in selling slaves and the Portuguese, to whom this institution was not new, saw nothing wrong in buying them. By the year 1444, there was a thriving market in African slaves in Portugal; in fact, when Columbus reached America some 50 years later, there were provinces in Portugal where the Africans outnumbered the Europeans. From a trickle of slaves at the beginning of the century, the traffic had assumed the proportions of a flood.

Still, this traffic might have petered out had it not been for the new impetus across the sea. Columbus had discovered America in 1492—an event, as we have seen, which unleashed waves of both greed and idealism in Europe. Unfortunately, greed seemed to have triumphed rather quickly in the New World. The lovely Caribbean islands, for example, proved to be ideal for the cultivation of sugar cane and other subtropical produce. Cultivation, however, demanded an enormous amount of labor. Where were the laborers to be found?

The answer seemed obvious. Put the people who lived on these islands to work—for the glory of God and the advancement of the sugar trade. Besides, they did not have guns, and if the good Lord had meant these people to defend themselves, He would surely have provided them with arms. So, the Spaniards put the native population to work with a vengeance. In less than 20 years after Columbus reached these shores, the "laughing, friendly, mild" people he had described to Queen Isabella were all but exterminated. Soon there was no one left to man the plantations.

The failure of the first colonizers to enslave the Indian inhabitants of their new possessions underscored the desirability of black servitude. So different was the Indians' cultural experience from that of their Spanish and Portuguese masters, they were utterly incapable of adjusting. There were, for example, countless reports of Indians who simply sat down and died for no apparent reason. Those Indians who were forced to work in the mines and plantations of the Caribbean islands died in huge number, if not from the oppressive labor, then from the diseases of the Europeans to which they lacked natural resistance.

That the African was better able to withstand these conditions is indicative, not of the lack of courage to resist captivity—his resistance was universally known and feared—but of his own cultural background and ability to absorb that of others. As we have already seen, African culture was not that different from the European. Africans did not, of course, take to slavery kindly, but they did not perish under it as did the West Indians. They were familiar with slavery as an institution; to a degree, they knew how to behave as slaves. Certainly, they knew how to survive as slaves. Within a comparatively short period, then, African slavery became a fixed institution of Iberian America. Slaves, first "seasoned" in the Caribbean islands, were soon introduced into the mainland possessions of Central and South America.

This commerce, which brought thousands upon thousands of Africans to the New World and which was later to flow northward to the English colonies, was, during its first century, almost exclusively limited to the Spanish and Portuguese possessions in America. The trade to the Americas opened formally in the year 1517, 25 years after the discovery of America by Columbus, when Bishop Las Casas advocated the practice of allowing Spaniards to import 12 African slaves each, to encourage immigration. It is known, however, to have existed prior to that year in the Western Hemisphere, in a less formal fashion.

Portugal was the first European country to take part in the African slave trade—the thousands of black slaves in Europe, before the discovery of America, had been carried there largely in Portuguese vessels. But it was early recognized that slavery in Europe could never be profitable, especially at a time when large numbers of European farm workers were themselves landless and seeking employment. Why bother importing slaves, when there was an ample supply of impoverished workers right at home? Only in the New World, with its vast natural resources, its desperate shortage of labor, and its vast undeveloped regions, would the slavery of Africans be profitable. And profitable it was. The demand for African slaves appeared to be limitless, and there was a whole continent from which to supply the demand.

Once the slave trade to the New World had begun in earnest, its lucrativeness attracted all those countries of Europe which could boast a ship. As a shipping venture it was a shipowner's dream—the perfect triangle. The boats carried trade goods to Africa from the home port; in Africa they took on a cargo of slaves; in the West Indies the slaves were bartered for sugar, spices, and molasses, which were brought back to the home port. Never an empty ship, and a handsome profit on every leg of the trade.

It is not surprising, then, that European nations fought each other for the privilege of managing the trade. Portuguese merchants, who monopolized the trade at the outset, proved to be no match for the government-sponsored companies of other nations. Soon, Dutch, French, English, Danish, and Prussian traders dotted the coast of West Africa with a series of forts and "factories." Spain, which was barred from Africa by a papal arbitration which gave her most of the New World, made her money by giving other countries a contract to supply her colonies with slaves. This contract, or *asiento,* was a rich prize for which all of Europe competed. In the eighteenth century, when England held the asiento, the slave trade was one of the most important aspects of

European commerce and the cause of most of her wars.

From the middle of the sixteenth century to the beginning of the nineteenth, England dominated the slave trade. At the height of the trade, in the eighteenth century, it is estimated that three-quarters of the ships flying the English flag were involved in slaving. American companies did not become an important factor in the trade until 1807, when England had abolished the operation. New England ships, however, were involved in the trade, on a small scale, as early as 1700.

The actual acquisition of slaves along the West African coast was an elaborate and complex process. Permanent trading posts—or "factories"—had to be established; treaties had to be made with the African kings; complicated bargaining sessions and exchanges between post officials and African officials had to be arranged. Finally, the slaves—war captives, criminals, political prisoners, and people who were merely kidnapped—had to be brought from the interior. Ships frequently had to make several stops along the coast in order to acquire a full cargo for the voyage west. All of this demanded organization, discipline, and cooperation. It is, therefore, not surprising that the trade came to dominate the commercial and social life of Africa—a monument to human greed and cruelty, both black and white.

For over 400 years, the slave trade flourished. Never before in history had it been possible to accumulate so much capital in so short a time. That wealth which accrued to the operators of the trade was often reinvested in the ironworks, mines, mills, and factories of Europe. Though it is difficult to determine the precise extent to which the slave trade spurred the industrial revolution in Europe, most historians agree that the role of the trade was critical. Eric Williams, in his book

Capitalism and Slavery, writes:

> The Western world is in danger of forgetting today what the
> Negro has contributed to Western civilization. Liverpool,
> London and Bristol, Bordeaux and Marseilles, Cadiz and
> Seville, Lisbon and Amsterdam, New England, all waxed fat on
> the profits of the trade in tropical produce raised by the Negro
> slave. Capitalism in England, France, Holland and colonial
> America received a double stimulation—from the manufacture
> of goods needed to exchange for slaves, woolen and cotton
> goods, copper and brass vessels, and the firearms, handcuffs,
> chains and torture instruments indispensable on the slave ships
> and slave plantations.... This contribution of the Negro has
> failed to receive adequate recognition. It is more than ever
> necessary to remember it today. England and France, Holland,
> Spain and Denmark, not to mention the United States, Brazil and
> other parts of South America are all indebted to Negro labor.

Indeed, the word "factory"—the very heart of the industrial
revolution—comes to us from the slave trade. Originally, a
factory was an African trading post, or fort, operated by a
"factor," or an agent or representative of a company, in which
slaves were gathered for export.

For the African kings and chieftains who supplied the
slaves to the factories, the trade was also a means for acquir-
ing wealth and power. The introduction of firearms, obtained
for bartered slaves, undermined the traditional power bal-
ances of African societies. Those nations that could obtain
the most firearms were able to raid more effectively and thus
further increase their wealth and power. In this fashion the
empires of the Ashanti, Yoruba, Dahomey and the Kongo were
enlarged and their new export economies established. The
records for Dahomey, the Kongo and other powerful African
kingdoms indicate that their armies were in a constant state
of war as they scoured neighboring areas in slave raids.

The "middle passage," as the voyage to the Caribbean came to be called, was replete with every form of misery known to man. Accounts of slave deaths due to overcrowding, disease, suicides, revolts, beatings, malnutrition, and mass murder are already well known and need not be repeated here. Suffice it to say that the slave trade reached a peak in the second half of the eighteenth century and that, by conservative estimate, upward of 14 million Africans were forcibly imported into the New World by the end of the traffic, in the late nineteenth century. It has also been estimated that for every African who reached these shores alive, four died either in the slave raids, the forced marches from the interior, or on board ship.

The predictable effect of this profitable business on Africa was a depopulated, demoralized, and ravaged continent. Over a period of some 400 years, Africa lost more than 60 million people—genocide on a scale unparalleled in human history. No one trusted anyone; old institutions and rules crumbled; all sense of security vanished. The great cities fell into disrepair, and some were abandoned. Jungle growth encroached upon the well-tended plantations and farms of Dahomey and the Kongo; roads disappeared. The civilized skills of bronze casting and carving deteriorated and were all but lost.

In a bizarre alchemy, undreamed of by the alchemists who sought to change lead into gold, the lifeblood of Africa was transformed into English factories and Dutch counting-houses; into an aristocratic American leisure-class society, described by Samuel Adams, New England Puritan, as:

> rich and in some ways sumptuous and curiously oriental. . . . In many families every child had his individual slave; great gentlemen almost openly kept their concubines; great ladies

half dozed through the long summer afternoons on their shaded piazzas mollified by the slow fanning of their black attendants, and by the laving of their feet in water periodically fetched anew from the spring house.

And yet, the slave trade must be understood in its historical context—as part of one of the cruelest periods in history. In the seventeenth and eighteenth centuries, life, everywhere, was cheap. Indeed, it was almost as if the whole world lived in a Nazi concentration camp. The cat-o'-nine-tails and the bullwhip, the hanging gibbet and the rack, the musket and the cannon were the symbols of law and order, the emblems of civilization. Laws, everywhere, were harsh and inhumane. A man, for example, could be hung for stealing a loaf of bread in all the civilized states of Europe and America. Indeed, in England, during this period, public hangings were probably the most popular spectator sport. According to eye witness reports, literally thousands upon thousands of people would gather in cities like London and Liverpool to watch the weekly hangings. Entire families gathered, men, women and children, to witness the death throes of the condemned.

If the life of a slave was cheap, so was that of a freeman —no matter what his color. The figures of the Liverpool slavers show, for example, that while the mortality rate among slaves on the "middle passage" was held to less than 20 percent—a higher rate would have been unprofitable—the mortality rate among "free" sailors averaged out to 47 percent. Indeed, this remorseless attrition of skilled English sailors was one of the principal reasons behind England's abolishment of the trade in 1807. England, who was so dependent upon her navies, was running out of sailors to man the ships.

To what extent this cruelty, this callous disregard for human life and suffering was a result of the traffic in human bodies is difficult to determine. No one, however, can deny that the brutalizing effects of the trade—which was so important to the industrial development of both Europe and America—permeated all of society. The gap between enslaving a black man and flogging a white sailor to death is not, after all, very wide. One made the other possible, if not inevitable. One cruelty gave birth to a hundred others.

And the echo of the slave trade is still heard today. During the 400 years that the trade flourished, it slowly, but surely, strangled Africa. Kingdom was set against kingdom, tribe against tribe, village against village. In Europe and America, though its effects were more subtle, they were no less disastrous. It left a legacy of brutality and callousness, of exploitation and guilt, and an artificial racial problem that remains explosive.

The injustice is eloquently described by W. E. B. Du Bois: "Raphael painted, Luther preached, Corneille wrote, and Milton sang; and through it all, for four hundred years, the dark captives wound to the sea amid the bleaching bones of the dead; for four hundred years the sharks followed the scurrying ships; for four hundred years America was strewn with the living and dying millions of a transplanted race."

4 The Song of Africa: Transplanted

During the course of the slave trade, some 14 million African immigrants survived to toil in the New World. The great bulk of these people, as we have already seen, was neither "savage" nor "primitive." For the most part, the families, societies, and cultures from which they were torn were highly developed and organized.

The great West African kingdoms, source of most of this vast immigration were civilized and well ordered, governed by a body of law and custom that had evolved over thousands of years. With the wealth produced by vast plantations, this agricultural people built great cities and courts long before the Europeans first made contact, in the fifteenth century. Also an artistic people, they supported and cherished a professional caste of artists, poets, sculptors, and musicians.

Indeed, the sculptors of West Africa, working in wood and clay, in bronze, and in gold and silver, established one of the most glorious and influential artistic traditions in the world. The creativity and the vision of these unknown artists continue to fascinate and influence art and artists to this day. Examples of their work are avidly sought by collectors and adorn museums all over the world.

It is in the realm of music, however, that the artistic genius of the West African people reached its highest development. Echoes of this tradition, as we shall see, dominate the popular musical expression of the entire world today; the energy and vitality of this African medium reach into the most remote areas of our globe.

It would be difficult to exaggerate the importance of music in West African life. It was part of religious ritual and a dominant element in royal pomp; it accompanied warriors to battle and workers in the fields. Music and its corollary, dance, were, in a very real sense, the very heart of African life.

An important aspect of this music, one that has been commonly overlooked, is that it was professional. All of the important West African kingdoms supported a sizable population of professional musicians and composers, who were organized into guilds. What this means, of course, is that musicians and composers were considered important enough by the society to be allowed the freedom to develop their art and perfect their techniques.

Although these music guilds tended to be family affairs, the music profession was, theoretically, open to all; anyone with the desire to make music could become a musician. However, in order to be admitted to the guild, the aspiring musician had to undergo a long period of professional training and apprenticeship. A series of rigorous tests demanded a familiarity with all of the instruments of West African music, which ranged from simple flutes to complex war trumpets; from violinlike stringed instruments played with a bow to harps, guitars, and banjolike plucked instruments; from a variety of xylophones, some of which were constructed on a curved frame with each key fitted with its own gourd resonator, to a staggering variety of drums, each with its own specific character and function. Thus, a boy whose father belonged to a guild had a decided advantage.

In this respect, African music was not very different from that in America today. Anyone can become a musician, but because it is an open profession, it is also highly competitive. In order to achieve professional status, the musician must demonstrate a mastery that can only be achieved through arduous practice and application. In this competition, the candidate from a musical family has an advantage over the one with a nonmusical background. Thus it is that most professional musicians tend to come from musical families.

The close alliance of African music and dance, mentioned before, can perhaps account for the development of a rhythmic virtuosity unrivaled anywhere—a virtuosity which, in turn, led to the most detailed and complete development of percussive instruments in the world. Nowhere do we find such a variety of drums and so many uses for these instruments. In West African music, orchestras consisting entirely of different types of drums were known to produce symphonies of elaborate rhythms and melody.

One of the most difficult to master was the "arm pressure" —descriptive of the method of playing—or "hourglass"—the resonating chamber was constructed in that form—drum. It had two drumheads, made of specially prepared calfskin, attached to each end of the hourglass by a network of leather thongs. The player beat the drumhead with a small curved stick while holding the instrument under his left arm in a manner that permitted him to tighten and relax the thongs and thus vary the pitch of the drum. A master player could develop a range of more than two octaves on this instrument, and when played in ensembles of from 5 to 12, the hourglass drum could produce both melodies and rhythms of remarkable subtlety and beauty.

Most drums were beaten with a stick, some with the palm of the hand; but there were still others that were not beaten at all. One of the most curious was the "friction" drum. This instrument was constructed out of a hollow log from a single species of mahogany. The drumhead was about eight inches across, but the body of the drum tapered so that the back was several inches narrower. Sound was produced by pulling on a foot-long reed attached to the inside of the drumhead by a small knob of leather. Holding the drum between his legs, drumhead down, and keeping his fingers moist by dipping into a gourd of water at his side, the player pulled the reed, letting it slip through his fingers with varying pressure. The vibration of the drumhead produced an awesome, roaring sound that could be heard for miles. The Dahomean word for playing this drum was the same as the word for milking a cow.

In addition to drums, there was also a variety of percussive metal instruments. Some of these were simple cymbals, which were clashed together or sounded by hitting with a stick. Others were complete sets of tuned bells in bronze or iron, arranged on a pole so that each bell was accessible for striking. Still other bells were scraped in order to produce a peculiar rasping sound.

Although drums and metal percussive instruments were

the fundamental elements in West African music, winds and stringed instruments were by no means neglected. At least a dozen varieties of harps were utilized, along with bowed instruments that produced a sustained, legato sound and plucked stringed instruments like the banjo and the guitar. Winds consisted of a variety of flutes, made of both wood and metal, trumpets, and bass horns.

All African instruments had a special symbolism associated with them. There was, for example, the *tabale,* a drum reserved for kings and great chiefs, whose sound was related to the spirits of light and water and to the speech of the people. An eight-string harp, as another example, had a special meaning for each of its strings; one tone meant "plenty" or "lack of plenty," another "light" or "dark," and so on. When playing this harp, the musician had to improvise not only a melody, but also a sequence of sounds that conveyed a logical meaning.

Although the West African musician who aspired to guild status had to be familiar with all of these instruments, he was expected to specialize on no more than one or two. However, in addition, he had to be a combination singer, composer and dancing master.

Despite the fact that there was no musical notation in West African music, there was a great body of secular and religious songs, dances, and music; this the professional musician was expected to learn by heart. All of the important rituals, for example, were made up of a traditional arrangement of songs and dances. The music for the occasion was then improvised within the framework of the sequence of the various songs, according to the inventive and improvisational talents of the individual musicians. Thus, while the music was ancient and traditional, it was also new, created at the moment out of the imaginations and musicality of the musicians who were performing.

As we have already seen in Chapter 2, African music is closely related to European music. The diatonic scale, for example, is common to both musics, and there is thus a similarity in the basic concepts of harmony. There are, however, great differences in these two musical traditions, as revealed in the treatment of the voice and in the employment of various sounds. Rasping sounds, as one example, were and are considered musical by West Africans—a factor which led to the development of a variety of instruments that utilized rasping sounds. Clicking sounds made in the throat, falsetto effects, and elaborate vocal slides or glissandos—all sounds not considered musical in the European tradition—are also conspicuous in African song.

The African conception of rhythm is, moreover, more complex and sophisticated than the European. In the European tradition different rhythms, as a rule, may be employed successively, but rarely simultaneously. A characteristic of African music, however, is just this simultaneous use of different rhythmic patterns. One musical statement may utilize three, sometimes four or five, different rhythmic patterns. A common rhythmic combination, still in use all over West Africa, has two percussion parts, one of which may be the beating of an hourglass drum, against a vocal section with an entirely different rhythmic pattern. Often, in more formal performance, there are several metrical patterns, each played by a drum of different size and tonal timbre. Chaos is avoided by the presence of an underlying beat that never varies. It is a style that imposes severe demands upon the performer. The musician had to develop an unfailing rhythmic sense in order to participate in West African music making.

At the heart of African rhythmic systems is the concept of tension. In contrast to European music, where the accents of a melody generally coincide with time beats, indicated by a baton or a handclap, the melodic accents in African music are generally in free rhythm. Although the melody itself may be tied to an underlying metronomic beat, this meter does not determine the rhythm. Musical tension is attained by deliberately staggering the main accented beats. In this manner, if two drums were to beat in triple time, the main emphasis of the second drum would fall on the second or third beat of the first drum's bar, never on its first beat. In practice, however, it is more common for the two drums to be playing in different meters, further staggering the main beats. When three drums are used, one performer beats out a simple triple or dual pattern while the lead drummer, utilizing any number of traditional metric patterns, creates spontaneous variations upon these patterns with great virtuosity, modifying them to suit the individual style of a dancer or singer. Meanwhile, the middle drum gives standard "replies" to the lead drum, the accents of which also cross those of the small drum. The performance, then, becomes a complex interweaving of melodic and rhythmic patterns, the inherent accents of which are in a constant state of tension.

This, then, was the music that came to America from West Africa. Although there were many different nations and tribes within this geographic area, with distinctive languages and customs, the music was remarkably homogeneous. Its principal characteristics can be summarized thus:

1. *Spontaneous creation.* While melodies and words of a song were traditional, they were not crystallized into a standard

form, but were modified at each performance by the creative genius of the musician or singer. This modification, it must be remembered, was not considered embellishment. It was a fundamental principle of West African music, which may be defined as free creation around a traditional framework.

2. *Melody.* The melodic structure of West African music was necessarily closely tied to the rise and fall of speech, for the languages were essentially "tonal" (the pitch of a spoken word determines its meaning). As a result, the development of a melody had to take meaning into account along with purely musical considerations; that is, in order to preserve the word sense in a song, the melody had to move up and down in conformity with the spoken word. This, of course, was a powerful inhibiting factor in the development of strict musical forms.

3. *Harmony.* In this area, West African music was not as well developed as the European. Harmonies in both instrumental and vocal performance tended to rely on simple progressions in thirds and fifths, while some areas restricted themselves to unison. Although there was little counterpoint, an antiphonal response pattern was typical of West African music. Thus, a lead singer or instrumentalist was answered by a choral response to produce rich and remarkably effective harmonic patterns.

4. *Rhythm.* In this area, as we have already seen, African music excelled. Percussive development was complex, subtle, and extremely sophisticated. It is interesting to note in this context, that black music in America did not reflect this African heritage very strongly. When we compare early New Orleans jazz, for example, with Afro-Cuban music, we cannot help but recognize the richer development of percussion in Afro-Cuban music. Gourds, rattles, bongo drums, tom-

toms, castanets, cowbells, and other percussive devices are liberally used in this expression, while the New Orleans music is limited to snare and base drum, embellished by a few cymbals. The reasons for this neglect in America will become clear shortly. Basically, it is attributable to the fact that the beating and construction of drums was prohibited by American slavers, who feared the use of these instruments as signals among scattered slaves.

Finally, the West African musician was also a principal means of communication. He was combination radio, telephone, and telegraph, sending messages over great distances by playing on drums and trumpets specifically designed for this purpose. This communication system was not based upon a code of dots or dashes like our own Morse code, but was based instead upon the musical elements of rhythm and melody. The signals sent out on these instruments were based upon the tones, patterns, and rhythms of language and closely followed ordinary patterns of speech. In this way, an accomplished musician could literally "talk" to another miles away.

This music and tradition came to America in the holds of the slave ships, along with the forcibly transported Africans. It was a rich tradition, sophisticated and highly developed, with unique concepts of sound and melody, of rhythm and the use of the voice. And in America, it was destined to play a dominant role in the creation of a distinctive national American music.

5 In America

So they came, snatched and stolen away from home and family. In the chafe of chains they came, packed into the rotting holds of leaking ships. Branded and whipped they came, stripped of dignity and freedom. In servitude they came, to be hewers of wood and bearers of water. For four hundred years they came, to try upon the shores of a new world.

All slavery was hell, but there were degrees of hell in the new world. Where they happened to be set ashore made a great difference in the lives of the human chattel that filled the holds of the slave ships. As Lerone Bennet, Jr. says in his book *Before the Mayflower:* "The slave trade was a stupendous roulette wheel. The boats fanned out from Africa and scattered human freight over the Western Hemisphere; around and around the wheel went, stopping here and there, sealing, wherever it stopped, the fate of mothers and fathers and their children to the nth generation."

Most historians agree that the Catholic colonies, especially those of Spain and Portugal, practiced a milder, more humane form of slavery than that which was administered in the British-Protestant colonies and later in the United States. For one thing, the Catholic church took an active interest in the lives of the slaves and effectively modified some of the fundamental cruelty of the institution. All Africans destined to toil in the Hispanic colonies were baptized and admitted to the sacraments of the church; their bodies might belong to their masters, but their souls belonged to God. Marriage among slaves, as one result of this practice, was recognized by both the church and the state and was held inviolate, as was the family. In Hispanic America it was illegal to break up a family through sale, as happened regularly in the British colonies and in the United States, after independence. In addition, the slave in the Catholic colonies frequently had some form of redress for his grievances under the law. In Brazil, for example, the sole function of one department of the government was to look after the rights and welfare of those in servitude.

Most important, however, were the laws of manumission—institutionalized procedures by which a slave might gain his freedom, independent of the whim of a master. Thus, any slave had the right to purchase his freedom. If he could earn his purchase price, his master had to accept payment, and the slave, by law, was free. In order to enable the slave to earn money, Sundays and a number of holidays were set aside.

On such days, those slaves who worked had to be paid for their labor and could keep the money earned. Another road to freedom was through childbearing. If slave parents had ten children in Hispanic America, the entire family went free. And once a slave gained freedom, he assumed all the rights and privileges of any other citizen.

It is perhaps because of these factors that a marked color bias never developed in these colonies. There were, of course, incidents of cruelty and inhumanity, but such cruelties appeared to have been directed toward the slave as a slave and not toward his race. As a result, the life of a slave in these colonies was less hopeless, less dehumanizing than the life of a slave in, say, the United States, where the Supreme Court—the highest tribunal in the land—ruled that "blacks had no rights that whites were bound to respect." And so, the "sorrow songs," the haunting, melancholy "spirituals," the "blues" did not come from Brazil or Cuba but from America, welling up out of the troubled hearts of blacks who toiled in Virginia, the Carolinas, Mississippi and Alabama. W. E. B. Du Bois, in *The Souls of Black Folk,* described this music thus:

> What are these songs, and what do they mean? I know little of music and can say nothing in technical phrase, but I know something of men, and knowing them, I know that these songs are the articulate message of the slave to the world....They are the music of an unhappy people, of the children of disappointment; they tell of death and suffering and unvoiced longing toward a truer world, of misty wanderings and hidden ways.

He then goes on to evaluate this gift of black music.

Little of beauty has America given the world save the rude

grandeur God himself stamped on her bosom; the human spirit in this new world has expressed itself in vigor and ingenuity rather than in beauty. And so by fateful chance the Negro folk-song—the rhythmic cry of the slave—stands today not simply as the sole American music, but as the most beautiful expression of human experience born this side the seas. It has been neglected, it has been, and is, half despised, and above all it still remains as the singular spiritual heritage of the nation and the greatest gift of the Negro people.

The history of this music begins properly in Jamestown, Virginia, in the month of August in the year 1619—one year before the Mayflower landed in Massachusetts. A Dutch man-of-war dropped anchor in the harbor, blown there by a storm at sea. Little is known of this ship other than that her captain was a Dutchman named Jope, her pilot an Englishman called Marmaduke, and her crew a mixed lot of cutthroats from all of the seafaring nations of the time. She was most probably a privateer—a pirate ship. Having apparently looted a Spanish ship somewhere on the high seas, her cargo included several African slaves, probably destined for the West Indies. This human cargo the captain offered to John Rolfe, leader of the Jamestown colony, in exchange for "victualle," or food. The transaction was arranged, and so some 20 blacks, with sonorous Spanish names like Isabella, Pedro, and Antony brought the first wave of Africa to the land that was to become the United States.

The most interesting thing about this initial wave of black immigrants was the fact that, strictly speaking, they were not slaves. To the inhabitants of Jamestown there was nothing unusual about the way the blacks arrived, for many of them had come in the same way—under duress and pressure. Under a system of indentured servitude that permitted poor white people to come to America by selling their services to the planters for a stipulated number of years, thousands of whites —paupers, thieves, prisoners, political dissenters, criminals, orphans—were shipped to the colonies and sold to the highest bidder. Many, if not most, did not sell their services voluntarily. Some were kidnapped on the streets of London, Liverpool, and Bristol, as the blacks were kidnapped in the cities and villages of Africa. Some were sold, as the blacks were sold, by the captains of ships.

In Jamestown, these African immigrants fit into this well-established system, which carried with it no implications of racial inferiority. That came later, much later. Like the majority of the white population, they were no more than indentured servants. They served their time in servitude and were then given their freedom together with a parcel of land to farm. In this way, blacks accumulated land, voted, testified in court, married, and were integrated into the society on a basis of complete equality. Some blacks prospered and bought black servants to work for them. At least one black imported and paid for a white servant whom he held in servitude. Kenneth M. Stampp, in his book *The Peculiar Institution,* described the prevailing social attitudes in early Jamestown. "Negro and white servants seemed to be remarkably unconcerned about their visible differences. They toiled together in the fields, fraternized during leisure hours, and, in and out of wedlock, collaborated in siring numerous progeny."

The American colonies in this period were, for the most part, poor and struggling, barely managing to survive in the face of the rigors of a wilderness continent. The economically important colonies were in the West Indies, where huge plantations had been organized to meet the worldwide demand of sugar. The enormous demand for labor was, of course, being fulfilled by African servitude. Eric Williams noted the ironic role that sugar thus played in history: "Strange that an article like sugar, so sweet and necessary to human existence, should have occasioned such crimes and bloodshed."

However if sugar was the villain in the West Indies, tobacco and cotton were soon to create the same role on mainland America. Here, again, were products for which a worldwide demand was growing; the prospects for making money were promising. Huge plantations were therefore organized to meet the demand. This development focused attention on the labor force. Who would work the fields? The great planters and plantation owners looked about them for a source of dependable, cheap labor. But why cheap labor? The answer is obvious: To grow wealthy in its exploitation.

Like the Spaniards before them in the West Indies, the rulers of the early American colonies were not too particular about the color or national origin of their work force. They tried Indian slavery, but this failed for the same reasons that it had failed the Spaniards. With no natural resistance to European diseases, Indians sickened and died upon close contact with whites; moreover, his cultural background made it all but impossible for an Indian to adjust to a life in servitude. Slavery of whites was also tried and abandoned. It was easy for a white slave to run off and blend into the general population, because, physically, there was no difference between the meanest white slave and the wealthiest planter. Besides, the supply of white slaves was limited. There simply were not enough available Irishmen and Englishmen to meet the demand, and other whites were under the protection of strong governments.

The choice then fell upon the blacks. Originally, it was a purely pragmatic choice that had nothing to do with race as such. Blacks did not sicken and die like the Indians. They were inexpensive and they were visible. They could run, but they could not hide. Finally, the supply seemed to be inexhaustible. Of course, certain attitudes among the general population—this business of equality and fraternization—would have to be changed. But these were not formidable obstacles. In a society riddled by class division, it would not be difficult to convince the poorest whites that they were better than blacks.

Still, it took decades to effect the desired sociological change. The weight of law had to be imposed before the degradation of the blacks was complete. Virginia and Maryland led the way, beginning in the late 1660s. Laws were enacted by the powerful landowners that made blacks servants for life—no more period of indentured servitude for them. Then, intermarriage between blacks and whites was forbidden by law. The children of black mothers were ruled free or bonded, according to the status of the mother. Finally, even religion was overruled, and the basis of servitude was shifted totally to race. In a law enacted in 1667, the Virginia legislature decreed that "the conferring of baptisme doth not alter the condition of the person as to his bondage or freedom."

During the next 30 years, law after law was enacted in the plantation colonies, each one designed to perpetuate the concept of racial slavery and racial inferiority. These laws stripped the black of all rights and made color the mark of servitude. More laws were then passed to guarantee this new black status. It became illegal to permit a black slave to learn how to read and write. More than five slaves were forbidden to gather without the presence of a white man. Slaves had to have signed passes from their masters when traveling abroad. A white man had the right—the duty—to stop any black and check his papers. Slaves were not permitted to testify in court. Slaves, of course, could not vote. From pulpits and journals, on street corners and markets, the planters spread the idea of racial inferiority. Africans were not only different than whites, they were also inferior. Ministers found justification for black servitude in the Bible. "The institution was ordained by God, Himself," they said. Learned doctors discussed the reduced cranial capacity of the African brain and its inability to benefit from higher education.

By the beginning of the eighteenth century, American slavery had evolved all of the legal apparatus that was to make the institution, as described by Kenneth Stampp, "the most oppressive form of slavery the world has ever known." It took some doing, but in the end the plantation owners succeeded. Not only did they manage to perpetuate the institution, but they also succeeded in squelching the last remnants of dignity and hope from their unfortunate chattel.

The black population of the mainland colonies grew slowly during the interim period of comparative freedom. But then, as the great plantations became more and more profitable, this population lunged forward. In the year 1665, when the first antiblack laws were being enacted, there were perhaps 25,000 blacks in the colonies. By 1710 the number had swelled to 75,000. When the Declaration of Independence was signed, there were some 750,000 blacks in America, the overwhelming majority of them slaves.

Unfortunately, we have little more than vague accounts concerning the music of these original black immigrants.

They were, as we have seen, integrated into the community and lived like the other colonists of the period, both as indentured servants and as free men and women. Certainly, they must have brought something of their African musical heritage with them to these shores, but since they represented only a small minority of the population and were not yet a people apart, not yet sojourners in the lands of their fathers, a separate musical identity did not emerge. They most probably picked up the music that was around them—the psalms of the religious services, the gigs, reels and ballads of secular life—and imbued it with something of their own African musicality.

But then, after the concept of black servitude became institutionalized by law, the life of the slave became cruelly circumscribed, his situation critically altered. The blacks then became a people apart, despised and abused by all. Systematically, they were deprived of all rights of personality. The sanctity of the family was ignored and children were sold from their mothers. Fatherhood, in effect, was ruled out for blacks, not just in matters of pragmatic convenience but by law. A Virginia court ruled that "the father of a slave is unknown to our law." A Mississippi court said that "the rape of a slave woman is an offense unknown to common or civil law."

It was under such harsh conditions that the blacks in America commonly lived, suffered, and survived. It was these conditions that gave birth to black music in America. Severely restricted by a cruel and immoral social situation, the blacks turned in upon themselves, ultimately to create a unique society within the confines of their isolation. This community found its voice and heart in music. A black man was not permitted to paint pictures—a waste of his valuable time; it was a crime to permit him to learn how to read and write; his historical and mythical African past were systematically obliterated. All he had left was music. Thus, all of the creative energy of this gifted people was funnelled into this one area. All of the longing, the yearning for peace and freedom found expression in the song of the slave.

It should not, then, be surprising that the black demonstrated marked musical ability. Not only were his inherent musical abilities honed by his social condition, but his selective capabilities were also sharpened and enhanced. The black slave approached music innocently in the sense that music served a purely creative function in his life. He was not influenced by snobbish or national appeal, nor could he consider music an individual accomplishment—something with which to impress his neighbors. For him music was a question of survival, nothing less. It was a collective expression, a communal effort; it was solace and inspiration —that art, which above all others, made the life of the slave humanly bearable.

Thus, the lowly black immigrant acted as a musical catalyst, borrowing from the music around him, from secular songs and dances as well as Protestant hymns and psalms. Because of his innocence, he was able to focus upon those aspects that had intrinsic musical value. This music, in turn, was enriched by his African heritage. It must be remembered that the African element was constantly being reinforced as new black immigrants arrived by the boatloads, by the thousands right up until 1860. The process was perfected and enhanced by a severely restricted creative energy that had its one outlet in music. In the harsh crucible of the slave warren, musical gold was being refined. It was not long before others recognized its value.

6 The Colonial Period

By the beginning of the eighteenth century, the oppressive legal apparatus of colonial American slavery was complete. The blacks who toiled in the mainland colonies were made a people apart, isolated from the rest of society, first by law, then by tradition and a racist ideology. They were a people stripped of hope and dignity, doomed to toil endlessly for the enrichment of those who owned them. For slavery was, after all, nothing more than a legalized form of robbery; it existed only because it was profitable to those who held control. The concepts of racism was merely a rationale.

As we have already seen, the slave master did everything possible to obliterate the African past of his unfortunate chattel. Since practical experience showed that homogeneous groups were better able to organize and execute revolts than a group of strangers, none of whom could speak the same language, fellow tribesmen and relatives were deliberately separated before the "middle passage" that brought them to America. A "breaking in" process of calculated brutality and terror, designed to cow the victim and render him docile and obedient, then completed the preparation of the unwilling African immigrant for life in the New World.

It was within such an oppressive legal and social situation that the black slave lived, toiled, and died. And it was out of this forced isolation that the black man created a unique community—a culture with its own language, traditions, practices, and mores. From the very beginning, music played a central role in this world; through it, we can trace the development of this American subculture.

At first, the music of the black slave was almost entirely African in derivation. In the desire to sing while working, one of the prime impulses in the growth of black music in America, the slave was merely reaffirming an age-old African tradition. In Africa, men sang at their work, and there was nothing to prevent them from doing the same in America. So long as they did their work, neither the plantation owner nor his overseer cared whether or not the slaves sang. In fact, singing came to be encouraged since it tended to lighten the burden and tedium of labor and thus make the slaves more docile and contented—which is to say, from the owner's point of view, less troublesome. If slave-ship captains encouraged their hapless passengers to sing on board, plantation over-seers had at least as much reason for doing likewise.

The emphasis placed upon the "spirituals" in popular con-ception has tended to overstress the religious factor in the development of black music in America. Although it is true that exposure to Protestant psalmody and hymnody had a direct influence on the course of Afro-American music and determined one direction it was to take, this was a gradual and comparatively late development. Christianity did not become a significant force in the lives of the blacks until the end of the eighteenth century. Unlike the Catholics in Latin America, the Protestant slave owners in the British colonies were not overly concerned about the souls of their chattel. The Reverend Samuel Davies, for example, estimated that in the year 1750 only about 1,000 blacks in Virginia, out of a population of about 120,000, had been converted and baptized.

The work song, then, of direct African derivation, was the first musical expression of the blacks in America. Here, in the cotton, tobacco, and rice fields, the toiling slaves worked to the accompaniment of song in an antiphonal lead and response style deeply rooted in tradition. Indeed, to this day few black musical activities come closer than work-singing to their original African counterparts. Today, though some of the melodies may be European in origin, the rhythms simple—dictated by the nature of the work being done—and the harmonic sounds no more African than European, the overall effect immediately calls to mind the work-songs of Jamaica, Haiti, and West Africa.

So important was the work song to the life of the slave, that the value of a good "singing leader" was quickly recognized. Such men commanded a premium price on the slave market, and advertisements often listed such accomplishments as an added inducement. The singing leader was as necessary to the work gang as the preacher was to the church.

Nor was the task of the singing leader simple. He had to

have a very special kind of talent—a feel for the work being done, together with an understanding of the men with whom he was working. In addition, he had to have the capacity to evoke both music and a physical, or motor, response. As in the dance, music and physical activity were inseparably joined; the song that captured the imagination of the workers, that engaged them, created a spirit that moved the work along. A good singing leader sensed what kind of song was needed at a given time and the best way to sing it. Often, he would improvise, not only melodies, but words.

Most of the early work songs came from Africa, but in time, a number of additional melodies were added to the reper-toire. A good many work songs were heard for the first time only a few moments after the events on which they com-mented took place. An important element, present in most black music, was the incidence of social criticism, ridicule, and protest in these songs. The substance of these songs ranged from the ribald to the devout, from the humorous to the sad, from the gentle to the biting. Some were downright irreverent, like this sample quoted by Lerone Bennet, Jr.

> Our father who is in heaven
> Whiteman owe me eleven, and pay me seven
> Thy kingdom come, thy will be done
> And if I hadn't taken that, I wouldn't have none

The instruments employed by black musicians during the early days of slavery were necessarily simple. They could not get African instruments and had to make do with what they found at hand. This, however, does not mean that their in-struments were "primitive"—"makeshift" devices inspired by irrepressible instincts to bang or twang on something. This view falls far short of the mark. A rustic, homemade banjo or fiddle, even if it had only one string, was, after all, a variation of an instrument with a sophisticated history. In truth, virtually every device used by black musicians, no matter how simple or makeshift it appeared, had its origin in African or European tradition. Very little was actually invented here, for there was no need to begin afresh with rudimentary, formless music or instruments. The African immigrant was stolen away from cultures that possessed a highly developed and sophisticated music. Indeed, they were conspicuously knowledgeable in this field and had well-defined concepts of the uses to which the voice and the sounds of various instruments could be put. In his music making in the New World, the black musician had merely to extract out of a storehouse of musical tradition.

The factors that go to make up a musical tradition are complex and varied. It is not only a question of musical scales and rhythmic concepts, but also, in a basic sense, of sound. It would appear that the range of instruments in a particular culture is determined, in part, at least, by traditional concepts of what sounds are appropriate to music. In West Africa, for example, scraping or scratching sounds were regarded as musical, and a variety of scraping instruments were thus developed for common use. (This African tradition is reflected in the New World use of scraping instruments that range from gourds and calabashes to the washboard of the traditional black "skat band.") When traditional instruments could not be obtained in the New World substitutes were found. Some, like the banjo, were highly sophisticated, while others were more elemental. But elemental instruments do not, in themselves, mean elemental music. Wood-block percussive devices are certainly primitive in a historical sense, but they are used in the symphony orchestra. If we think of brass horns and trumpets as a category of highly developed instruments to which the African was exposed in America during colonial days, it is worth remembering that horns and trumpets of many kinds were widespread in Africa long before the first slave cargoes sailed for the New World.

A typical example of this kind of development is the washtub bass or "gut bucket," which together with the washboard are commonly seen in black "skat bands." At first sight, this ungainly instrument appears to be makeshift in the extreme. The washtub bass, however, has a venerable history; forms of the instrument were reported as early as the beginning of the eighteenth century. It is, basically, an upside down washtub (or appropriate substitute) with a cord attached to the middle of the base. The other end of the chord is attached to a stout stick, the free end of which is then braced against the lip of the inverted tub so that the string is held taut. Plucking or slapping the cord produces a musical tone, the tub acting as a resonating chamber. Pressure against the stick varies the tautness of the cord and produces tones of different pitch. It is used primarily as a percussive instrument that produces bass tones. The tub player stands with one foot on its edge to hold the instrument firmly in the ground. A second player, at times, beats a rhythm on the metal head with sticks.

This instrument is an improvisation only in the sense that available materials were adapted to an old use. The ancestor of the washtub bass is found not only in West and Central Africa, but also in black communities in the West Indies and in South America. The original African device was apparently a development of the spring snare, used for capturing small game. In its most primitive form, it was a kind of earth bow, fashioned by digging a hole in the ground next to a small sapling, pegging a bark or hide membrane over it, then bending the sapling and fastening it by cord to the center of the membrane. One man would play the taut cord by rubbing, plucking, and slapping it, while a second player beat a rhythm on the membrane with sticks. Later, portable variations used carved wooden boxes instead of the hole in the ground for resonating chambers.

The morphology of the American washtub bass leaves little doubt of its African ancestry. Not only was the basic structure of the instrument similar, but the manner of playing was also virtually identical to the African technique. Add to this the frequently seen second player beating on the drumhead with sticks and it is difficult not to conclude that the makeshift tub is in reality a sophisticated instrument with a long history behind its development.

The same circumstances hold true for many of the other "makeshift" instruments used by black musicians in colonial America. Metal kettles and pans, as another example, were commonly used as percussive instruments. But again, these devices were anything but haphazard. Certain specific sound qualities were demanded of each piece of "hardware," and there was a standard of what was good sound and what was bad that could be explained only through the existence of a tradition. This tradition, of course, derived from West Africa, where metal percussion was, and is, an important element in music. Throughout this area, forged iron bells were used as percussion elements; some, in fact, were highly developed instruments. One type, for example, played by striking the bell with a metal rod, could produce as many as seven notes in the hands of a skillful player, and double and even triple bell arrangements were frequently used. Where bells were not available, bits of resonant metal were employed. Seen in this light, the kettles, fry pans, and pots, used singly, in groups of two or three, or in combination with other instruments, can be considered descendants of these earlier instruments rather than makeshift, improvised noisemakers.

Insofar as these improvised instruments reveal a direct relationship to African originals, their use in America, first by blacks and then by white musicians, serves to trace the influence that black music exerted upon the developing music of America. Thomas Jefferson, for example, in his *Notes On Virginia*, stated that "in music they [blacks] are more generally gifted than whites, with accurate ears for tune and time, and they have been found capable of imagining a small catch. ... The instrument proper to them is the banjar, which they brought hither from Africa, and which is the original of the guitar, its chords being precisely the four lower chords of the guitar." This, of course, is the instrument which came to be known as the banjo and played such an important role in American music.

Exercising that remarkable aptitude for music that Jefferson and others observed, black musicians in America soon learned to play European instruments. In some cases, slaves employed as household servants were encouraged to develop musical skills that might contribute to the pleasure or social prestige of their masters. Such skill was reflected in the price of a slave. In 1753, for example, *The Virginia Gazette* carried an advertisement offering to pay a premium price for an "orderly Negro or mulatto who can play well the violin." The same paper also printed a notice offering for sale "a young, healthy Negro fellow...who plays extremely well on the French horn." Still another announcement offered a reward for a runaway slave "who took his fiddle with him."

The influence of African music was noted as early as 1753. A description of a Richmond ball that was printed in *The*

Virginia Gazette described the music of Sy Gilliat and London Briggs, two black musicians who "belonged" to the household of Baron Botetourt, later Governor General of the colony: "To the music of Gilliat's fiddle and Brigg's flute, all sorts of capers were cut...sometimes a *Congo* was danced and then the music grew fast and furious when a jig climaxed the evening." The *Congo* mentioned in the report was nothing more than a modified version of an African ritual dance, which was performed by blacks throughout the eighteenth and nineteenth centuries all over the New World. The dance was described by Lafcadio Hearn more than 100 years later, after he saw it danced in New Orleans in 1858. It is interesting to note that a version was also danced by the dandies of colonial Virginia society. What this suggests is that black music was already making inroads into American musical expression in this period. The fact that a congo was danced at a fancy colonial ball in Virginia indicates that black music must have already been well established in broad segments of society.

An interesting side development is seen in American children's ring games and playparty songs. Actually, examples of such game songs occur all over the world; few children anywhere are without them in some form or another. In the United States today ring games and playparty songs of English and French origin are common, but there are also many that cannot be traced to any European source and are most certainly derived from African models.

Children's ring and line games were old hat to African children in the New World, for they had a remarkably rich repertoire of African originals to fall back upon. What is significant here is that the black children brought traditional African musical concepts to bear upon the songs, endowing them with a distinctive imagery and often lending to the postures and motions of the accompanying action the characteristics of black dancing. In time, of course, various songs and games from the white culture were absorbed. However, many such songs were altered, improvised upon, and reshaped to the extent that they lost their European character altogether.

A typical American ring-game song was recorded recently by Folkways Records. Although it was sung by white children in the rural south, its African character is immediately apparent in the way it was sung, the rhythms, and the words. In this game, every player has a number. When his number is called by the leader, he must respond with an appropriate answer and then pass the play on to another player. Should a player become rattled and give the wrong response or miss his turn, he is called out and is out of the game. His number cannot be called again. Should some player call this number, he too is ruled out. The words are half sung, or called, with stylized inflections, to the accompaniment of rhythmic clapping.

> Group: One two three and a zing zang, zing
> Leader: Number three
> Number three: Who, me?
> Leader: Yes, you.
> Number three: Couldn't be.
> Leader: Then who?
> Number three: Number nine.
> Number nine: Who me?
> Leader: Yes, you.
> Number nine: Couldn't be.
> Leader: Then who?
> Number nine: Number four.
> And so on.

In the same way that European elements were absorbed

into the children's ring games, similar secular elements were absorbed into the mainstream of black music. In time, the music that grew out of the fusion of these two sources came to take on a distinct character that was neither European nor African. It was a new music that could only have come to flower under the peculiar conditions of the blacks in America.

The second important influence on this developing music was religious in nature. As we have already seen, the British-Protestant slave owners were not overscrupulous about the souls of their chattel. A writer in the *Athenian Oracle* of London, in 1705, expressed what was probably a common attitude: "Talk to a planter of the soul of a Negro, and he'll be apt to tell you that the body of one of them may be worth twenty Pounds, but the Souls of an hundred of them would not yield him one farthing."

In time, however, these attitudes changed. In the mid-eighteenth century a number of evangelical sects became active throughout the British colonies. The most prominent were the Baptists and Methodists, who conducted revival meetings all over the country. In their zeal, they did not ignore the black slaves. The blacks, in turn, took readily to the fervor and freedom, the ecstasy and exuberance of revivalism. Here was a religion that spoke to them of hope and brotherhood. They could readily identify with Moses and the Israelites who were slaves in Egypt.

Among the most active preachers of the gospel to the blacks was the Reverend John Davies of Virginia, a follower of John Wesley, founder of Methodism. In his journals, Wesley tells of receiving letters from Davies describing his work among the black slaves. It is interesting to note that in all of these letters, the Reverend Davies makes significant references to music. One letter states:

I have supplied them to the utmost of my ability with books. They are exceedingly delighted with Watts Songs. And I cannot but observe, that the Negroes, above all of the human species that I ever knew, have the nicest ear for music. They have a kind of ecstatic delight in psalmody; nor are there any books they so soon learn, or take so much pleasure in, as those used in that heavenly part of divine worship.

In an other letter, dated 1752, the Reverend Davies wrote:

For some time after, the poor slaves, whenever they could get an hour's leisure, hurried away to me, and received them [books] with all the genuine indication of passionate gratitude. All the books were very acceptable but none more so than the Psalms and Hymns, which enabled them to gratify their peculiar taste for psalmody. Sundry of them lodged all night in my kitchen; and sometimes when I have awakened at two or three in the morning, a torrent of sacred psalmody poured into my chamber. In this exercise some of them spend the whole night.

This emphatic corroboration of the musical aptitude of the blacks is impressive. More important, however, this eyewitness account gives us a startling insight into the genesis of the spiritual, more so than any amount of theorizing. From these accounts, our imaginations can readily reconstruct the atmosphere of emotionalism and fervor, the tears, the heartfelt outpourings of emotion that must have taken place at these meetings. We can almost feel the delight taken with Hymns and Psalms in the anthology of Dr. Watts. The blacks responded wholeheartedly to their direct appeal to the emotions. They took an ecstatic pleasure in the surge of communal song and in the sense of spiritual and physical satisfaction that came from expressing themselves freely. There was an innate talent that not even the harsh conditions of slavery could repress.

It must be remembered, however, as we trace the growth and development of Afro-American music, that there was no uniform development, just as there was no uniformity of conditions under which the blacks lived. There was, rather, a variety of social and cultural conditions, ranging from the comparative sophistication of urbanized blacks living in the cities to the primitive plantation life of the Georgia Sea Islands. Here, blacks living in relative isolation retained definite Africanisms in their speech and customs for generation after generation. Afro-American music, as it exists today, has taken from them all; it is the product of a fusion, a process of acculturation, that encompassed elements from all phases of life in the New World. It was the musical genius of the blacks that gave shape and form to this music, lending it a character and feel that is completely distinctive and unique. Thus, though the spirituals originated in an Anglo-American tradition, they were transformed at the hands of unknown black composers, imbued with a musical breath and sweep that were completely lacking in the original.

7 Independence

During the second half of the eighteenth century, strange ideas were stirring all over Europe and the New World. People everywhere were thinking and questioning; young people were restless and impatient. As old ideas and values crumbled, institutions that had been accepted for centuries were suddenly suspect and under attack. New religious groups sprang up everywhere, and new prophets and leaders arose to redefine the accepted relationships between man and God and man and man.

How do we explain this restlessness that gripped so much of the world during this period, this restlessness destined to reach a climax in revolution and upheaval, the effects of which are felt to this day? Perhaps it stemmed from a new industrialism, which was rapidly transforming the very landscape of the world; from new processes and techniques, which were altering age-old patterns of work and social relationships. Perhaps it was prompted by the New World, with its vast empty spaces and its even vaster potential. Perhaps it grew out of the burgeoning natural sciences, which were beginning to unravel some of the great mysteries of nature and, in the process, altering the position and role of man in the universe.

However it came about, a new spirit was abroad that excited youth everywhere and frightened their elders. It was almost as if Europe paused for a moment in its busy plunder of the world to look about and think. Out of this turmoil came a wave of idealism that was to carry all of mankind, eventually, to a new level of dignity and freedom.

In the British colonies in the New World, this spirit reached a shattering climax in the War for Independence. Prompted by this new idealism, the people of colonial America revolted against a colonial rule that they found oppressive and tyrannical. "Liberty and Equality" were the slogans under which the war was fought and won; "all men are created equal," proclaimed the Declaration of Independence. The black slave, hearing these brave words, must have thrilled with new hope and determination. For no man in the New World valued freedom more; no man had more regard for liberty and equality.

How did enlightened Americans, who fought the oppression of England, view slavery during this period? After all, here was a colony, with 750,000 of its people in bondage, about to go to war in support of a theory that "all men are created equal and endowed by their Creator with certain inalienable Rights, that among these are Life, Liberty and the pursuit of Happiness."

Certainly the men who drafted the Declaration of Independence gave thought to this aspect of their society. Thomas Jefferson inserted a clause in the Declaration condemning the institution, but it was struck out in deference to slaveholders. That Jefferson fought to keep the clause in is, however, doubtful, for he was also a slaveholder and shared in many of the racist concepts of his time. Patrick Henry, another Virginian and Revolutionary War hero, was perhaps more honest than most. In a revealing letter to a friend, Henry expressed his views on slavery.

> Every thinking honest man rejects it [slavery] in speculation, how few in practice. Would anyone believe that I am Master of slaves of my own purchase? I am drawn along by ye general Inconvenience of living without them; I will not, I cannot justify it.

He, at least, did not stoop to rationalizing his injustice by resorting to racist concepts. Patrick Henry's sister Elizabeth, of more sturdy conscience, perhaps, freed all of her slaves before the revolution with the unequivocating declaration that: "it is both sinful and unjust, as they are by nature equally free as myself, to continue them in slavery."

As far as the blacks themselves were concerned, "freedom" and "liberty" were magic words. It is not surprising that they rallied to the new flag of rebellion and were in the forefront of the agitation that preceded open rebellion. Blacks, for example, were prominent participants in the tumultuous Stamp Act riots, which rocked the colonies in the decade before the war. An unsympathetic Boston resident, John Miller, described one of these riots: "For a fortnight the tension in Boston continued to increase until, on the night of August 28, 1765, boys and Negroes began to build bonfires in King Street and blow the dreaded whistle and horn that sent the Boston mob swarming out of taverns, houses and garrets. A large crowd gathered around the bonfires, bawling for 'liberty and property.' "

On March 5, 1770, Crispus Attucks, a free black sailor, was the first American to fall in the famed Boston Massacre that was so instrumental in bringing about the Revolutionary War. Black militiamen fought alongside whites at the battles of Lexington and Concord and helped defend Breed's Hill, in the battle mistakenly called Bunker Hill. One of the outstanding heroes of that encounter was Peter Salem, a black soldier who is reported to have shot Major Pitcairn, the British commander. Another black, Salem Poor, a lieutenant in the militia, was commended after the battle for having "behaved like an experienced officer, as well as an excellent soldier. To set forth particulars of his conduct would be tedius...in the person of this Negro centres a brave and gallant soldier."

The Battle of Bunker Hill was fought in June 1775. In July, General George Washington of Virginia assumed command of the Revolutionary Army and one of his first acts was an order barring the enlistment of blacks in the Continental Army. Several factors entered into this decision. A major consideration, of course, was the fact that so much of American agriculture was dependent upon slave labor, especially in the plantations of the southern colonies. Another argument held that the practice could be dangerous to the revolutionary cause. If America used black troops, the British were certain to follow suit.

As it turned out, the order proved to be academic. In

November 1775, Lord Dunmore, the deposed Royal Governor of Virginia, took a step that forced Washington to reconsider. From his ship in Norfolk Harbor, Lord Dunmore offered freedom to all male slaves who would bear arms against the rebels. As was to be expected, thousands of slaves immediately deserted their masters in response to this opportunity for freedom. Their first battle, at Kemp's Landing in Virginia, was a decisive victory for these newly freed blacks; a black battalion succeeded in routing a unit of Virginians. As the white rebels broke ranks and ran, their former slaves gave chase. In one of the supreme ironies of this paradoxical war, a black soldier captured his former master and marched him back to the British line at the point of a saber. Victory must have been doubly sweet for that particular soldier, if somewhat confusing. His ex-master had been, after all, fighting for "freedom."

The action of Lord Dunmore compelled Washington to revoke his order barring black enlistees in the Continental Army. His new decision was that blacks who had fought in the early battles could join the ranks of the rebels. However, the order that was ultimately issued bore the further stipulation, appended by Congress, that only free blacks could join; slaves continued to be barred from the ranks—again, in deference to the large slaveholders of the plantation states.

But circumstances of war intervened once more. For one thing, the Revolution was not very popular with the colonists; indeed, it is questionable whether the revolutionaries ever commanded a majority of the population. There were large numbers of Loyalists in all the states who opposed the war and actively supported the British against what they considered "rebellious traitors," and a great many people who did not care one way or the other so long as they were able to pursue their own lives.

In any event, Washington and the Continental Congress had a hard time enlisting men to fight for the Revolution. Although there were some one million men of fighting age in America at the time, the Revolutionary Army was never more than 50,000 strong—most of the time, much smaller. Bounties of land and money were offered to lure volunteers, and some states even offered slaves; but still enlistees were in short supply. General Washington himself despaired: "Such a dearth of public spirit, such stock-jobbing and fertility in the low arts to obtain advantage of one kind or another, I never saw before, and I pray God I may never witness again. Such a dirty mercenary spirit pervades the whole that I should not be at all surprised at any disaster that may happen."

The winter of 1777 marked the low point of the war, as far as the revolutionary cause was concerned. General Washington came to Valley Forge that winter with an army of 9,000 men. By the spring of 1778, there were 6,000. One-third of General Washington's army had deserted.

After Valley Forge, the Continental Army had no choice. The desperate need for soldiers dictated a change in policy. Thus, all able-bodied men—black or white, slave or free— were welcome. In January 1778, General Washington petitioned the Rhode Island Assembly to authorize the enlistment of black slaves from that state. In February, the Assembly took this precedent-shattering step. Two months later, Massachusetts did the same.

After this, blacks played a prominent role in all phases of the Revolutionary War, some 6,000 coming under arms. They participated in all the major battles of the war, fighting as soldiers, sailors, and as spies. Along with such other foreign heroes as Lafayette and Kosciusko, a contingent of black soldiers from Haiti, called the Fontages Legion, answered Washington's call for help. At the siege of Savannah, this group was instrumental in preventing a rout of the American forces.

After the surrender of Cornwallis at Yorktown, a wave of democratic idealism swept America. Thousands of the staunchest Loyalists left with the British, emigrating to Canada and the West Indies. Those who did not take sides in the war now gave their enthusiastic support to the victors. But no matter; a new republic had been born, paid for by the blood and valor of her sons, both black and white. And both reaped the rewards of victory. It has been estimated that more than 100,000 blacks gained freedom as a direct result of the Revolutionary War. Herbert Aptheker, the noted black historian, estimates that at least 100,000 more "voted with their feet," making their way to Canada, the wilderness areas of Florida, and the western frontier during the chaos of war.

In the years immediately following the defeat of the British, the magic of the Declaration of Independence infected almost everyone. Thousands of blacks were manumitted in this enthusiasm. Typical was the action of Philip Graham, a wealthy Maryland landowner. He freed all of his slaves in 1787, saying, "Holding his fellow men in bondage and slavery is repugnant to the golden law of God and the unalienable right of mankind as well as to every principle of the late glorious revolution which has taken place in America."

In the northern states, free blacks agitated and petitioned against the institution of slavery. They brought suits in the courts and organized demonstrations in the streets. As the result of one such suit, brought to court in 1783, slavery was ruled illegal in Massachusetts because of the words "all men are created equal" in the state's Bill of Rights. In the preamble to the act for the abolition of slavery in the state of Pennsylvania, Pennsylvanians were called upon to give proof of their gratitude for deliverance from the oppression of England by "extending freedom to those of a different color by the work of the same Almighty hand." And as, in state after state, by legislative decree and by court decision, black slaves were declared free men, slavery gradually died in the North.

For a time, it seemed that America was really going to be America, with "Liberty and Justice for All." Everywhere the spirit of democracy made itself felt. Slavery was dead in the North and all signs showed that it was dying in the South. It appeared that men of good will might solve the racial dilemma once and for all. Baptists, Methodists, and Quakers joined to condemn the institution and agitated against it. Blacks like Joshua Bishop of Virginia and Lemuel Haynes of Connecticut were appointed pastors of white churches. A black astronomer-mathematician named Benjamin Banneker helped survey the site that was to become Washington, D.C.; and the poems of a black girl who was born in Africa, Phyllis Wheately, were the vogue and were being read everywhere. Her book of poems was the first published work by a black woman and the second by an American woman in the New World.

Then, everything changed. The dream proved to be stillborn. America was not destined to be America, not just yet. Two events occurred that were to have a climactic effect upon all Americans.

One of these events, oddly enough, was a second Revolutionary War for Independence. This war, however, was fought, not by white merchants and landowners, but by black slaves, on the French island of Haiti, or Santo Domingo as the Spanish called it, in the West Indies. There, slaves led by Toussaint L'Ouverture, himself an ex-slave, successfully overthrew the French in 1791, in a brilliant, decisive, and bloody campaign. Toussaint then proceeded to defeat both an English and a Spanish army, which were dispatched to the island to help the French landowners.

By all accounts, Toussaint was a remarkable leader. Not only was he a brilliant general, but he was also a statesman of broad vision and compassion. His aim was to transform Haiti into a multiracial state, and, toward that end, he succeeded in establishing a working alliance with the whites on the island. Under a constitution inspired by that of the United States, blacks and whites joined together to build a new state.

After Napoleon came to power in France, however, a free Haiti was looked upon as a threat to the French Empire. Napoleon therefore dispatched an army under the command of his brother-in-law, Victor Emanuel LeClerc, to oust the black leader. Toussaint and his black legions fought the French to a standstill. Then, tricked by an offer from the French to negotiate, Toussaint was captured and hauled away to France. He died in April 1803, in a cell in a medieval fortress in the Jura Alps, on the French-Swiss border.

With the capture of Toussaint, leadership of the Haitians fell to Jean-Jacques Dessalines, who had fought at the side of the fallen leader. In a series of pitched battles, Dessalines' armies completely routed the French. When LeClerc surrendered to him outside Le Cap, Dessalines, more implacable than Toussaint, is said to have ripped the white out of the surrendered French tricolor and raised the remaining red and blue banner to proclaim the second republic in the Western Hemisphere.

Napoleon, who had nurtured ambitions for a French slave empire in the New World, was compelled to reconsider. He had lost some 60,000 men and a rich colony. Thus, in 1803, he sold the Louisiana Territory to the United States for $15 million—less than four cents an acre, the greatest real estate bargain in history—abandoning his New World project.

News of the black victories and atrocities in Haiti sent shudders of fear through the plantation South. Every hint, every rumor of slave disaffection brought to mind the specter of burning, pillaged houses and slaughtered whites. And as the fear of the slave grew, this fear, in turn, engendered a wave of cruel repression.

The second pivotal event was rather different in character, though equally potent in effect. Its prime mover was an itinerant Yankee teacher and tinkerer named Eli Whitney.

Whitney was born in Westboro, Massachusetts, in 1765, to a family of farmers. Quick to learn and possessed of a flair for mechanics, he did not choose to remain on the farm. Instead, he continued his studies at Yale College in New Haven, from where he was graduated in 1792. After graduating, he accepted a position as tutor in the Savannah, Georgia, household of Mrs. Nathaniel Greene, widow of the Revolutionary War hero. Here, at a dinner party one evening, he met a group of planters who were discussing the need for a machine that could separate the short staple upland cotton from its seed. Cotton, at the time, was a relatively minor crop. For, though cotton cloth was being woven, it was so expensive an item it was a luxury that few could afford. The labor necessary to separate the seed from the lint was the cause of the prohibitive cost.

Eli Whitney, with his flair for mechanics, applied himself to the problem, and within a few weeks he produced a model "cotton gin." This device consisted of a wooden cylinder encircled by rows of slender spikes, set a half-inch apart, which passed between the bars of a grid. The grid was so arranged that seeds were held back as the lint was pulled through by the revolving spikes. A revolving brush then cleaned the lint from the spikes, and the seeds fell into another compartment. A man, operating the machine alone, could clean 50 pounds of cotton a day; by hand, it would take ten men the same amount of time to accomplish the task. A patent for the device was granted on March 14, 1794.

It was a simple device, but its consequences were enormous. Overnight, the South found a new, profitable crop. With the aid of the "gin," cotton cloth could be made cheaper than woolens. What was once a luxury for the few was suddenly available to all. Weaving mills in England and New England expanded to meet the demand, and in the South, where the plantations of Virginia, the Carolinas, Georgia were quick to respond to the lure of wealth, cotton became king. All thoughts of equality and democracy were forgotten as slave labor was put to work growing and processing cotton. Greed raised its head and ideals were shunted aside. America was to be a land of liberty, but not for all, not just yet.

For the blacks in America, the brief, heady moment of hope was squashed. In a reaction that is still difficult to understand, an entire population seemingly turned against them. Free blacks in the North were insulted and attacked on the streets, and laws were promulgated to restrict their movements and opportunities. In the South, the voice of the racist was loud, and the shackles of bondage were tightened everywhere. Indeed, the slave states took on the aspect of an armed camp in a frenzy of repression designed to guarantee the subjugation of the slave. Cotton was king, and the blacks groaned under a new tyranny. Once more, the black community was isolated from the rest of society. Once more, the blacks turned in upon themselves in disappointment and heartbreak.

In the slave warrens of the United States, the "sorrow" songs and the "spirituals" blossomed and bore fruit of haunting beauty. Out of this experience, out of this disappointment, frustration, and sorrow, black and unknown bards distilled a poetry and a music that had a message for all mankind. During the nineteenth century, between two wars, black music grew, expanded, took on a breadth and scope that expressed the longing for peace and freedom of all humanity. It was this poignant, human quality that lent black American music its unique texture and depth.

Black bards sang of a sun that had ceased to be a friend.

> Oh, the sun will never go down
> go down
> Oh, the sun will never go down
> The flowers are bloomin' forever more
> Oh, the sun will never go down
> go down

They sang of tears.

> I know moon-rise; I know star-rise
> Lay this body down
> I walk in the moon-light; I walk in the star-light
> To lay this body down
> I'll walk in the grave yard; I'll walk through the grave yard
> To lay this body down

> I'll lie in the grave and stretch out my arms;
> Lay this body down
> I go to judgment in the evening of the day
> When I lay this body down
> And my soul and your soul shall meet in the day
> When I lay this body down.

When Thomas Wentworth Higginson, who commanded a black regiment in the Civil War, first heard this spiritual, the experience sent shivers running down his back. "Never, it seems to me," he said, "since man first lived and suffered, was his infinite longing for peace uttered more plaintively."

Black bards sang defiance.

> When Israel was in Egypt's land
>   Let my people go
> Oppressed so hard they could not stand
>   Let my people go
> Go down, Moses, way down in Egypt's land
>   Tell old Pharaoh, let my people go.
> No more shall they in bondage toil
>   Let my people go.
> Let them come out with Egypt's spoils
>   Let my people go.

A tradition based upon the recollections of former slaves identifies Harriet Tubman, the black antislavery fighter and unofficial conductor of the Underground Railway, as the Moses of the song. Whether the tradition is accurate or not makes little difference. The first 60 years of the nineteenth century in America were a period of defiance and agitation among the slaves. Gabriel Prosser, Nat Turner, Denmark Vesey — all led rebellions that shook the South of its lethargy. Runaway slaves and the Underground Railway were debated in Congress and the question was considered time and again by the Supreme Court. It was the period when Frederick Douglass raised his voice in thunder against the hypocrisy of his native land. More than ever before, the South was an armed camp, where planters slept with guns under their pillows, in fear of their slaves. No more revealing picture of the spirit of the times can be found than in a glance through some of the southern periodicals. All carried pages of advertisements for whips, chains, collars, thumbscrews, bits designed for the human mouth, harnesses, handcuffs, ankle chains, and such other agricultural implements as were deemed necessary to get a day's work out of the reluctant slaves.

And, in spite of everything, black bards also sang of joy.

> Well, you got shoes, I got shoes
> All of God's children got shoes, got shoes
> And when I get to heaven, goin' to try on my shoes
> I'M GOIN' TO SHOUT ALL OVER GOD'S HEAVEN!

How were these songs composed? An answer was quoted in a book of *Slave Songs of the United States,* published in 1867, attributed to Joyce Miller McKim.

I asked one of these blacks, where they got these songs.
"Dey make 'em, sah."
"How do you make them?"
After a pause, evidently casting about for an explanation, he said:
"I'll tell you; it's dis way: My master call me up an' order me a short peck of corn and a hundred lash. My friends see it and is sorry for me. When dey come to de praise meeting that night dey sing about it. Some's very good singers and know how; and dey work it in, work it in, you know, till dey get it right; and dat's de way."

A more scholarly explanation was offered by the musicologist M. Kolinski, who made a comparative study of some 130 spirituals and West African songs. He found that "thirty-six spirituals are either identical or closely related in scale and mode to West African songs. The spiritual 'Cyan Ride' has an almost exact counterpart in a Nigerian song, and 'No More Auction Block' is clearly the same as one of the Ashanti songs."

Kolinski then went on to discuss such musical esoterica as pendular thirds, linear combinations of fourths, binary meters, rubato figures, triplets, and offbeat phrases. He concluded that while many of the spirituals were evidently patterned after European melodies, some without distortion, they were all either altered so as to conform, or selected for adoption because they already did conform to West African musical patterns. The spirituals, then, are an ideal example of musical syncretism—the coming together of compatible traditions.

8 Between Two Wars

For the blacks, the promise of the Revolution was squashed. It had been overrun by a machine, "a thing of brushes and cylinders and wire teeth," in the words of Lerone Bennet, Jr., "that made black men and white fibers big business." In one of the great ironies of history, the American War for Independence turned out to be an instrument for the extension of slavery. England abolished the institution in 1807 and freed all slaves under English jurisdiction. In America, the Emancipation Proclamation was not issued until January 1, 1863—55 years later.

What was this period like? Ulrich B. Phillips, an apologist for slavery, described life in the ante-bellum South as idyllic.

The plantation was pageant and variety show in alternation. The procession of plowmen at evening, slouched crosswise on their mules; the dance in the new sugarhouse, preceded by prayer; the bonfire in the quarter with contests in clogs, cakewalks and charlestons whose fascinations were as yet undiscovered by the great world; the work songs in solo and refrain, with not too fast a rhythm; the baptizing in the creek, with lively demonstrations from the "sisters" as they came dripping out; the torchlight pursuit of 'possum and 'coon, with full-voiced halloo to baying houn' dog and yelping cur; the rabbit-hunt, the log-rolling, the house-raising, the husking bee, the children's play, all punctuated plantation life—and most of them were highly vocal. A funeral now and then of some prominent slave would bring festive sorrowing or the death of a beloved master an outburst of emotion.

This, of course, is the magnolia blossom, mint-julep South of *Gone With the Wind*. Unfortunately, it never existed outside the imaginations of a few dreamers, though the dream was accepted for a time as history by nearly everyone. Modern historical scholarship has largely destroyed that myth, however, and a more realistic view now prevails that paints a far different picture. The historian Stanley M. Elkins, for example, concluded that "the only mass experience that Western people have had within recorded history comparable in any way with Negro slavery in America was undergone in the nether world of Nazism. The concentration camp was not only a perverted slave system; it was also—what is less obvious but even more to the point—a perverted patriarchy." Kenneth M. Stampp, another historian, described the institution as "a social system as coercive as any yet known erected on a foundation of the most implacable race-consciousness yet observed in virtually any society."

The most eloquent descriptions, however, were offered by the slaves themselves. "Slavery time was tough, boss. You just don't know how tough it was," said Tines Kendricks, an ex-slave. Another recalled the attitude toward black children on the plantation where he had lived. "Children had to go to the field before they were six years old. Maybe they don't do nothing but pick up stones and tote water, but they got to get used to being there. Old master used to sit in the shade looking at the children going to the field and say, 'Slave young, slave long.' "

Though a parasite upon the backs of the oppressed blacks, the ante-bellum South supported an oddly gracious and aristocratic society. It centered about the manor houses of the large plantations — the "big house," in the slave vernacular. Here, great ladies and gentlemen spent their days in idle luxury and their evenings at stately balls and elaborate dinner parties. An obsessive topic of conversation was slavery and slaves. White planters and their ladies would trade stories and chuckle over the "childish" antics of their blacks; some envied them their carefree, happy-go-lucky existence. They then went to bed with pistols under their pillows.

Among the more "childish" antics of the contented slaves was a delight with fire. Throughout the South, houses, barns, crops, and stores burned with discouraging regularity. Things got so bad that it became difficult for a southern homeowner to get insurance. In a letter addressed to a resident of Savannah, Georgia, dated February 17, 1820, the director of a Philadelphia based insurance company, turned down a request: "I have received your letter of the 7th instant respecting the insurance of your house and furniture in Savannah. In answer thereto, I am to inform you, that this company, for the present, decline making insurance in any of the slave states."

In reality, this period was a time of agitation and revolt.

In the North, the abolitionists were a constant irritant to the national conscience. In the South, slave leaders like Nat Turner, Gabriel Prosser, Denmark Vesey, and others organized and led revolts. It was the time of the Underground Railway, and each year thousands of slaves "voted with their feet" and escaped to freedom in Canada and the wilderness areas of America. Indeed, the question of runaway slaves rocked the nation. It was debated in Congress and the Supreme Court, but it was never successfully resolved. Human beings proved to be a stubbornly recalcitrant form of "private property."

The English, who had abolished slavery in 1807, delighted in reminding American "republicans" about their hypocrisy. Runaway slaves and abolitionists from the United States were welcomed and lionized in England. They were invited to speak and their memoirs were published and avidly read. It reached a point where slave narratives became a dominant subject in English letters. One critic observed that "America has the mournful honor of adding a new department to the literature of civilization—the autobiographies of escaped slaves."

Arrayed against the slave, was all the power of the state, the law, the militia, the police, and the U. S. Army. All participated in the mass robbery that was slavery. During this period, blacks were robbed of their labor, their freedom, their families, their dignity and, finally, to make the score complete, their music.

As we have already seen, the blacks in their isolation and oppression were developing a remarkable music. And around this time it became associated with one of the most bizarre and grotesque forms of popular entertainment the world has ever seen. In the slave quarters of the great plantations, a unique culture had come to life that centered primarily upon music. An important feature of this culture came to be called the "Jubilee," a slave celebration that usually accompanied the periodic distribution of clothes, prizes, and favors and generally took place on holidays or other festive occasions. All the people of the plantation—black and white—participated in the festivities, and over the years a distinctive pageant of music, dance, and comedy evolved about the celebration.

Though the origins of the Jubilee are obscure, it was already well established in the colonial period. Shephard N. Edwards, born in Tennessee of slave parents, has handed down this description as he heard it from his parents.

> It was generally on Sundays, when there was little work, that the slaves both young and old would dress up in hand-me-down finery to do a high-kicking, prancing walk-around. They did a take-off on the high manners of the white folks in the "big house," but their masters gathered around to watch the fun, missed the point. It's supposed to be that the custom of a prize started with the master giving a cake to the couple that did the proudest, most original movement.

Basically, the Jubilee was valued as an entertainment. Since most of the plantations that supported a sizable slave population were large—many of them encompassed thousands of acres—and, like miniature kingdoms, were isolated from one another by vast distances and inadequate transportation facilities, they tended to be self-sufficient economic units. In the early period, everything needed for life—food, clothing, building materials, tools—was produced on the plantation; even later, it was just luxuries and fineries that were imported.

All life thus revolved around the land—around the rotation of the seasons, the planting and reaping, the tilling of the soil. This was, after all, the source of all wealth. Only holidays, festivals, and because they were rare, visits eased the monotony of this existence.

On the occasion of a visit—whether a "neighbor" or a relative just arrived by ship from England—gentlemen amateurs would commonly bring out their violins, flutes, harpsichords, and French horns and perform the classic works of European masters. In the ballroom of the "big house" a stately minuet would be danced to celebrate the event, and perhaps a "racy" waltz—if the group were daring.

But then, after the genteel entertainment had been finished, the party would move out to the lawn, where the slaves would perform a show of their own. Here was a different music and a different approach to singing and dancing, which was looked upon by the people of the "big house" with tolerant amusement. It was all very "primitive," yet the infectious rhythms, the songs, the high-stepping dance, and walk-around of the black field hands exerted an irresistible fascination, and so the Jubilee was a featured part of all important social occasions.

In fact, so effective was this celebration in terms of entertainment, it was copied on the stage. Oddly enough, the first accounts we have of professional performances of this kind come to us from England. Perhaps an Englishman connected with the theater saw a Jubilee and recognized its potential for the stage. However it came about, there began to appear in English music halls, during the last decades of the eighteenth century, acts in which whites impersonated blacks. In these performances white entertainers, their faces darkened with burnt cork, sang in an exaggerated black dialect and

The "Jubilee," a traditional slave celebration of many southern plantations, produced a music that was to have a dominant influence upon
American musical expression. *(The Bettman Archive)*

This lithograph, circa 1840, shows the traditional instruments and assemblage of the minstrel show which gained immense popularity in America in the two decades preceding the Civil War. *(The Bettman Archive)*

Dan Bryant, one of the most famous minstrels to appear in "blackface" is seen in this daguerreotype. *(The Bettman Archive)*

Slave deck of the barque "Wildfire," captured by the U.S. steamer "Mohawk," is from a woodcut that appeared in an American newspaper circa 1860. A steady flow of forced immigrants helped reinforce and keep alive an African tradition in American music. *(The Bettman Archive)*

The Fish Jubilee Chorus toured America and Europe in the 1870s, singing traditional spirituals and songs. Their performances helped introduce black American music to the world. *(The Bettman Archive)*

New Orleans marching band. Such bands, organized in New Orleans after the Civil War, were one of the principal precursors of jazz. *(United Press International Photo)*

danced to tunes they called "plantation melodies." The practice, however, never became a vogue in England, and entertainers in "blackface" disappeared from the stage.

In America, blackface entertainment by white performers
apparently did not begin until the beginning of the second
decade of the nineteenth century. However, when it did
surface, this kind of theatrical fare became increasingly popular. Performers like George Washington Dixon and "Daddy"
Rice performed in music halls, singing and dancing in blackface to the accompaniment of banjo and bones—both of
which had originated in the black community. (The bones
were nothing more than two flattened bones or sticks held
in the fingers of the closed fist and snapped together with a
rolling motion of the wrist to produce remarkably varied
percussive effects.) Though, at first, their acts were simply
programs of songs and dances that aped the music and movements of plantation blacks, over the years these individual
acts merged into a wholly unique and novel theatrical form
of immense vitality, which captured the imagination of the
American public. They laid the foundations for what was to
become the minstrel show.

The prototype for the classic minstrel show, which was to
have a marked influence upon all subsequent American popular music, made its debut in New York City, in February
1843, at the Bowery Amphitheatre. "The novel, grotesque,
and surpassingly melodious Ethiopian Band, entitled, Virginia Minstrels" was advertised as "an exclusively minstrel
entertainment, entirely exempt from the vulgarities and other
objectionable features which have hitherto characterized
Negro extravaganzas." It would thus appear that "Negro Extravaganzas" were already a familiar form of theatrical entertainment in the year 1843 and that the Virginia Minstrels

were organized to exploit a form that was already popular.

The cast of this group was made up of four performers, all of whom had theatrical experience: Daniel Decatur Emmett, who played the violin and was to achieve a degree of immortality with his composition of "Dixie"; Billy Whitlock, banjo; Frank Bower, bones; and Richard Pelham, tambourine. Dressed in exaggerated costumes, wearing white trousers, calico shirts, and long swallow-tailed jackets, their faces blackened with burnt cork, the Virginia Minstrels made their debut. On stage they proceeded to entertain a delighted audience with a shrewd combination of singing, dancing, dialect patter, and instrumental music.

The most important feature of this troupe was this association of four performers as a coordinated team, each playing a characteristic instrument and comic role, that presented a complete, self-contained show. Four-man teams became the standard cast of the minstrel show which sprang to immense popularity in the two decades preceding the Civil War.

Three years later, in 1847, a second minstrel show, organized by Edwin P. Christy and called *Christy's Minstrels,* opened at Palmo's Opera House in New York City. So successful was this production that the next year Christy leased Mechanic's Hall on Broadway, where the troupe stayed on for ten years. Christy also claimed to have organized the first true minstrel show in Buffalo, New York, in 1842.

Although the origins of the minstrel show are vague, these two companies undoubtedly established the pattern that was to dominate the form throughout the nineteenth century. Characteristically, the performance was divided into two acts. In the first act the performers were arranged in a semi-circle on the stage: the "Interlocutor," a kind of straight man, was seated in the center, in whiteface and full dress;

at either end of the semicircle were the endmen, "Mr. Tambo," who played the tambourine, and "Mr. Bones," who played bones. The production opened with a chorus as the performers made their "grand entrance," marching around the stage in imitation of the plantation cakewalk. At the conclusion of the march, the Interlocutor gave the command, "Gentlemen be seated." Then followed a series of jokes and gags between the Interlocutor and the endmen, interspersed with ballads, comic songs, and instrumental numbers played chiefly on the violin and banjo to the accompaniment of tambourine and bones. Each member of the company was given an opportunity to display his talents in song, dance, and comedy. The second act was called the "olio" and was made up of a series of individual routines, a farce in which the entire cast joined in, burlesque opera, and more dialect jokes. The "grand finale" was a singing-dancing number, called the "walk-around," in which each member did a specialty while the others sang and clapped hands.

Although modified and altered by different companies, this was the classic form of the minstrel show as it was performed on the American stage. After 1860, the shows became more lavish and spectacular, and in the 1870s, it was not unusual to have as many as 100 performers in a troupe. Such productions were called "gigantean," "mammoth," "gargantuan," and "extravaganzas."

Musically, the minstrel was a typical American mixture of sources and traditions. The basic influence was undoubtedly that of the southern black, of the plantation slave. This aspect of the minstrel was discussed by Francis Pendleton Gaines, in his book *The Southern Plantation.*

> Most writers agree that in its beginnings American minstrelsy ... endeavored to reproduce the life of the plantation darkey.

The songs sung by the Ethiopian serenaders were reminiscences of the songs heard where the Negro was at work, on the river steamboat, in the sugar-field, or at the camp-meeting.... It is likely that the steamboats of the Mississippi and the Ohio, as well as the southern plantation, were the direct source of many of the Negro tunes and songs that found their way into the repertoire of the earliest blackface entertainers, such as Dixon, Rice and Emmett. The river was a great carrier of songs, and many Negroes worked on the river.

This music, which was taken from the blacks, was altered and modified on the stage by performers who were mostly white. In this music, then, we can trace a derivation that could have occurred only in America. Minstrel music, the popularity of which swept the nation and even affected peoples in Europe and South America, was an Anglo-American modification of an Afro-American modification of African, English, Scotch, Irish, German, French, and Spanish originals.

At its best, minstrel music was full of vitality and exuberance on the one hand, and poignant sentimentality on the other. Many of its songs have withstood the test of time and are still heard and sung today. Probably the most influential of the minstrel composers were Daniel Decatur Emmett, who wrote "Dixie" (in New York City, incidentally), and, of course, Stephen Foster. Songs by both have achieved the status of national folk music.

In one sense, however, the "Ethiopian business," as minstrelsy was called, was a tragic development, another example of the exploitation of the blacks in America by whites. It borrowed freely from a musical idiom that originated in a true musical genius while it degraded the originators. All over America people flocked to watch performers impersonate blacks in the most vile caricatures. The conventional form of the minstrel, with its Interlocutor and two stooges with tambourine and bones, crystallized the white myth of the grinning, lazy, good-for-nothing, yet innocently happy "darky." Indeed, "Jim Crow," the title of an early minstrel song, became descriptive of the social and economic oppression of the blacks.

Part of the popularity of the minstrel show must be attributed to guilt. America, after all, was supposed to be a republic with "liberty and justice" for all. Statesmen wrestled with this contradiction and so did the man in the street. It must have been comforting, then, to go to the theater and watch the fake blacks project an image of "happy," "shiftless" darkies. See how they sing and dance and laugh. They don't mind slavery, not really. Everything is all right. Besides, the music was nice. It set your feet to tapping and your voice to singing.

For almost 70 years blackface minstrels dominated the American musical theater, bringing to birth and keeping alive a vast body of popular music, the vitality and exuberance of which were recognized by all. It represented the first great wave of music that flowed out of the black experience into the mainstream of American cultural life.

By 1850, there were at least 75 companies performing minstrel shows in theaters all over America. The minstrel reached California with the forty-niners during the gold rush. One company, headed by Henry Whitby, toured South America. Another brought the "plantation melodies" to Europe where they met resounding acclaim. By 1860, the number of minstrel troupes had doubled.

Then, after 1870, the popularity of the minstrel show began to wane. It practically disappeared as a theatrical form by the beginning of the twentieth century, though it remained an influence in popular entertainment. Al Jolson and Eddie Cantor, for example, appeared in blackface as late as the 1920s and early 1930s.

It is interesting to note in this context that the minstrel show died along with slavery. It reached immense popularity in the decade before the Civil War, but then after Emancipation its popularity faded. Within ten years, it had all but disappeared from the popular stage. The minstrel, however, was instrumental in uncovering a rich vein of music. It brought to the whole of America, and to a good part of the rest of the world as well, a new and unique approach to song and dance whose influence was destined to dominate all aspects of American music in the next century.

9 Emancipation

Slavery was not an issue in the war. President Lincoln said it time and time again. The question was union, the survival of this association of United States as a viable nation. Slavery had nothing to do with it. Even after the first pitched battle of the war—the Battle of Bull Run, on July 21, 1861, in which Union troops were routed—Congress attempted to maintain this fiction. The very day after the battle, on July 22, 1861, Congress declared that the federal government had no intention of interfering with slavery. This question was not an issue in the war.

But it was an issue. Indeed, it was the central issue in this bloody war between the states. Only the politicians, it seemed, were ignorant of this. Free blacks in the North were well aware of the stakes and rallied to the flag in response to Lincoln's call for men who loved the union. From all over the North—from Boston, Philadelphia, New York, Cleveland, Chicago, Hartford—black volunteers came forward and organized. They hired halls, drilled, and formed military units like the Hannibal Guards of Pittsburgh and the Crispus Attucks Guard of Albany, Ohio. Dr. G. P. Miller, a black physician of Battle Creek, Michigan, sought authority to raise an army of "5,000 to 10,000 free men to report in sixty days to take any position that may be assigned to us." However, the Lincoln administration thanked the volunteers and sent them home. The presence of black troops in the Union lines, it was felt, would confuse the issues in the war. Slavery was not one of them.

But to the black slaves in the South, as to the free blacks in the North, slavery was an issue. No one invited them and no one asked them, but masses of fugitive slaves kept escaping into Union lines. Indeed, they constituted a continuing problem for commanders in the field. Some Union commanders returned them to their masters, but still the fugitives came. John C. Fremont, commanding Union troops in Missouri, recognized the potential in this black support and issued a proclamation freeing the slaves of Missouri rebels; however, Lincoln immediately revoked it. But Ben Butler, of Massachusetts, who commanded a regiment in Virginia, welcomed fugitive slaves into his lines and was upheld in his action by Congress. He chose to consider them "contraband of war"—a choice phrase, since it said nothing about slavery. "Contraband," thereafter, could be freed.

For almost two years, Lincoln maintained the official fiction that the war was nothing more than a polite misunderstanding between white gentlemen, a war that had nothing to do with either blacks or slavery. "My paramount objective in this struggle is to save the Union," Lincoln said in August, 1862, "and is not either to save or destroy slavery . . . What I do about slavery and the colored race, I do because I believe it helps save the Union, and what I forbear I forbear because I do not believe it would help save the Union."

Within a year, however, this policy was changed, but not because of Union humanitarianism or love of democracy. It was changed because of the brilliance of rebel generals and fighting men. In battle after battle, Confederate troops outfought, outmaneuvered and outgeneraled the Union forces. The South, it must be remembered, was vastly outnumbered as far as men and materiel were concerned. Twenty-three states were arrayed against 11; and the white population of the former (22,000,000) was four times that of the latter (5,500,000), though, in truth, this figure did not reflect the labor of some 3,700,000 black slaves—a vital element in the South's capacity to make war.

Both sides had had to create armies before they could fight. Here the South had a distinct advantage. Among the officers who resigned their commissions to join the Confederacy were a disproportionately large number of the ablest men in the old army. The two Johnstons, Joseph E. and Albert S., and Robert E. Lee had been preeminent in their profession; indeed, Lee had been offered command of the Union armies. Moreover, Jefferson Davis, president of the Confederacy, was a graduate of West Point and had served with distinction in the Mexican War. His experience enabled him to appoint the best officers to command his armies and to see that the first steps in military organization were wisely taken.

Lincoln, on the other hand, had little military experience.

He had no basis for judging the competence and professional merits of his officers, and he had personal acquaintance with few soldiers. His appointments were thus often made for political reasons. All of these factors were reflected on the battlefields during the first two years of the war. The Union general staff had to be proven in battle, and it took time to separate the good from the bad.

Another advantage of the South was that Southerners could be more quickly trained as soldiers. As we have already seen, the South had always been something of an armed camp as a result of slavery. Most white Southerners were accustomed to bearing arms and were familiar with violence, and so the use of guns and horses in war was easily taught. In addition, there was in the South an aristocracy accustomed to rule, together with a poorer class of whites who recognized the aristocracy's claim to leadership. In the North, on the other hand, the army had to be recruited principally from people who lived in cities and from poor European immigrants. There was also a strong tradition of libertarianism in the North and many soldiers found it difficult to adapt to the despotism of military discipline.

Finally, Southerners knew exactly what they were fighting for. The aristocrats were fighting to preserve a way of life. They were fighting to preserve slavery, the institution from which all of their status derived. There was no talk of morality or principle. Privilege was at stake and all other considerations paled before this question. Indeed, some Southerners denounced the Declaration of Independence and demanded that not only free blacks be enslaved, but poor whites as well. The poor whites, in turn, flocked to the rebel cause to preserve the precious illusion that they were, at least, better than the blacks. In South Carolina a law was passed compelling free blacks to wear diamond-shaped badges.

The North with its obvious advantage of men and materiel, expected a quick victory over the rebels. After Fort Sumter, Lincoln called for 75,000 militiamen for three months' service, while Davis, the Confederate president, called for 100,000. Apparently, neither Davis nor Lincoln foresaw the dimensions the war would assume. In the first years of the war, Robert E. Lee, Johnston, and Beauregard, with the other rebel generals, taught the North that war was, indeed, hell.

In order to win, the North needed to muster all the resources at its command. One of the most obvious were free blacks in the North and black slaves in the South. In the summer of 1862, Lincoln despaired of the Union cause. "Things had gone from bad to worse," he wrote, "until I felt that we had reached the end of our rope on the plan of operations we had been pursuing; that we had about played our last card." He knew that a meeting of northern governors at Altoona, Pennsylvania, would demand emancipation and the use of black soldiers in the Union armies. Therefore, on the eve of the governors' conference, Lincoln issued the proclamation that changed the entire character of the war. No longer would it be fought under the slogan of "Unity." The new rallying cry was "Freedom."

Actually, the Emancipation Proclamation (issued September 22, 1862, to take effect on January 1, 1863) had little immediate practical effect since it applied only to states that were in rebellion and therefore beyond federal control. Slavery was not actually abolished in the United States until Congress adopted the Thirteenth Amendment, in December 1865. Its political effect however, was immediate and widespread. Blacks throughout the North and South flocked to the flag. Some 70,000 served in the Union ranks, both as soldiers and as sailors. In the South, the message reached into every slave cabin and every black work brigade, and hundreds of thousands of men, women, and children went looking for President Lincoln's soldiers. John Eaton, a newspaper reporter, described the migration as "the oncoming of cities . . . a slave population rising up and leaving its ancient bondage, forsaking its local traditions and all the associations and attractions of the old plantation life, coming garbed in rags or in silks, with feet shod or bleeding, individually or in families and larger groups."

And they came singing, with new words to a melody that has since been identified as an ancient Ashanti war song that had somehow remained alive and virtually unchanged over the generations.

> No more master's horn for me
> No more, no more
> No more master's horn for me
> Many thousands gone
> No more driver's lash for me
> No more, No more
> No more driver's lash for me
> Many thousands gone.

After 1863, black soldiers fought gallantly in all of the major battles of the war. In one such action, fought in a suburb of Richmond, Virginia, on September 29, 1864, a black division was charged with the task of securing a Confederate stronghold on New Market Heights. It was an all but impossible task. The stronghold was heavily fortified and rebel artillery commanded the narrow stretch of land over which the Union soldiers had to charge. There were also two barricades of felled trees with sharpened points facing the attackers. The soldiers would have to cross a brook and a stretch of open land, charge uphill under artillery and musket fire, break through first one and then the second barricade before they could reach the rebel trenches.

The black soldiers charged, their columns raked by grapeshot and cannister. They reached the first barricade under the withering fire, and axemen hacked through the logs. Then the second, stepping over the bodies of their dead and wounded. Again, a hole was opened and the men poured through the opening. Within a half hour the battle was over. Black men in blue uniforms stormed over the trenches, and the defenders broke ranks and ran. It had been a bloody 30-minutes' work; behind the victors on the hill lay the bodies of 543 of their comrades. Twelve black soldiers were to be awarded the Congressional Medal of Honor for their deeds that day, in that battle.

The war dragged on for another year. Finally, the tattered remnants of the Confederate armies surrendered at Appomattox, on April 9, 1865. The war had been won and the Union was preserved. In December of that year, Congress ratified the Thirteenth Amendment, and slavery in the United States was abolished. A new question now faced the nation. What was to be done with the ex-slaves? A strange phenomenon was occurring throughout the South. Ex-slaves by the hundreds of thousands were wandering about the countryside savoring their first taste of freedom.

The life of the slave had been severely restricted. Most slaves, unless they were sold, rarely left the confines of their home plantations. Many lived and died without ever having gone more than ten miles from the spot where they were born. It has been estimated that the average slave rarely came into contact with more than 50 people in a lifetime. Thus, with a need born of centuries of such close confinement, hundreds of thousands of blacks throughout the South simply wandered. They filled the roads and flocked to the cities and towns. What was to be done with them? Frederick Douglass, the great black abolitionist, had an answer. "Do nothing with him," he thundered.

> Your doing with him is their greatest misfortune. The Negro should have been let alone in Africa... let alone when the pirates and robbers offered him for sale in our Christian slave markets... let alone by the courts, judges, politicians, legislators, slave drivers... If you see him plowing in the open field, levelling the forest, at work with spade, rake or hoe—let him alone; he has a right to work. If you see him on his way to school, with spelling book, geography and arithmetic in his hands—let him alone.... If you see him on the way to the ballot-box to vote—let him alone.

For a time, in the flush of victory and idealism that followed the war, America even tried democracy. Blacks were permitted to vote in the elections of 1867 and 1868, and the results were astonishing. An ex-slave, and a woman at that, Blanche Dilso Bruce, was elected senator in Mississippi. Pinckney Benton Stewart Pinchback was governor of Louisiana. In South Carolina, a black was elected lieutenant governor. In Florida, the secretary of state was an ex-slave, and a black judge sat on the bench of the state Supreme Court in North Carolina. Blacks were sheriffs, superintendents of education, state treasurers, mayors, and post office officials. A total of seven blacks entered Congress as duly elected representatives.

Blacks and whites went to school together, ate in restaurants together, worked together, rode street cars together, and voted together. An interracial board governed the University of South Carolina, where a black professor, Richard T. Greener, taught white and black students metaphysics and logic.

The amazing thing about this period was the almost complete absence of any feeling of vindictiveness on the part of the blacks. They appeared to have been more than willing to let bygones be bygones. In the state legislatures, black politicians passed the most progressive legislation that America had ever known. Schools, hospitals, civil rights guarantees were all championed by ex-slaves for the benefit of all citizens—black and white.

All of these things, and more, took place in America during the ten years of Reconstruction (1867–1877). It seemed for a time that America was really going to be America, after all. W.E.B. Du Bois called this period the "mystic years." Unfortunately, they were not destined to last. Powerful economic forces had been unleashed by the Civil War, and the United States emerged from this conflict with the industrial capacity to alter the balance of power in the world. In the North, a great class of industrialists dubbed the "Robber Barons," had laid the foundations for great wealth and international influence. Accordingly, to the South was delegated the role of breadbasket and producer of raw materials for the nation. "Cheap labor" was again the rallying cry, and democracy was to take a seat in the "back of the bus" once more.

In all of this turmoil and upheaval, how did black music fare? The appropriate answer is that in response to even this limited degree of freedom it exploded. In one of the great cultural rebirths in all of human history, black music in America grew, expanded, and overflowed into the cultural life of the nation, in wave after wave of sound that continues to this day. In the years immediately following the Civil War, the first musical wave came in the form of the spiritual. During the war, the North met the southern slave face to face and heart to heart for the first time and was thus introduced to the true "plantation melody," as distinct from the debased caricature of the minstrel stage. In the "Black Belt" of the deep South, they found a people who had been touched only lightly by the world about them. Their appearance was uncouth, their language, in many instances, strange and barely intelligible, but their hearts were human and their singing stirred men with a mighty power.

In Port Royal, near the sea islands of the Carolinas, Thomas Wentworth Higginson heard them and felt shivers run up and down his back. And it was here, in a school established by the Freedman's Bureau, that Lucy McKim Garrison came to teach and stayed to learn—an experience that resulted, in 1867, in the publication of the first collection of spirituals, under the title *Slave Songs of the United States*. Only the words and tunes were printed, without any attempt at harmonization, but the volume remains an important primary source.

The editors, Miss Garrison was one, were aware of the difficulties they faced in publication. They had heard the blacks singing these spirituals in their original form, and they made it clear in their notes that their musical notation could only approximate, not accurately reproduce, the true music in actual performance. "It is difficult to express the entire character of these Negro ballads by mere musical notes and signs. The odd turns made in the throat and the curious rhythmic effect produced by single voices chiming in at different irregular intervals seem almost as impossible to place on the score as the singing of birds or the tones of an aeolian harp."

In Nashville, Tennessee, George L. White, who was born in Cadiz, New York, and had fought in the battles of Chancellorsville and Gettysburg, also heard the song of the blacks. He, too, was employed by the Freedman's Bureau and taught school. He, too, stayed to learn. So impressed was he by the music of his black students, he organized a chorus that the world might share it with him. In 1871, the Fisk Jubilee Singers—made up of four ill-clothed black boys and five girl-women—began a tour that was to last seven years.

They sang in Cincinnati and Cleveland, in Washington and New York, and everywhere their reception was the same. Many people came to scoff at these "black minstrels," but listening to their song, they stayed to cheer. Then their songs carried the Jubilee Singers across the sea. They sang in England, Scotland, Ireland, Holland, France, and Germany. They sang before Queen and Kaiser, lords and commonfolk. All responded to the power of the music that came forth from these nine black throats. After seven years of traveling and singing, they brought back a hundred and fifty-thousand dollars to found Fisk University.

For a time, in the first decades following the Civil War, the Jubilee chorus was widely imitated. A number of similar choruses appeared in the concert halls and meeting places of the United States. Some of these groups, such as the singers of Atlanta and Hampton, were excellent, but some offered only a pale shadow of this authentic black music. Nevertheless, the spiritual became firmly rooted in the mainstream of American music as a result of this first great wave of black music, and an end was finally put to the minstrel show as a dominant form of popular entertainment. For anyone who had heard the dramatic and powerful singing of the good black choruses, the minstrel, with its gross caricatures and exaggerated impersonations of "plantation darkies," lost any appeal it might have had.

The great vogue that the spirituals enjoyed in the decades following the Civil War was short-lived. Reconstruction, with its promise of democracy and reform, gave way to a new wave of black repression. In the South, blacks were systematically stripped of their newly won rights by a resurgence of racism. In the North, people were growing weary of the strife and agitation. They wanted no more than to go back to work. The blacks would have to get along as best they could, as far as they were concerned.

The black choruses that brought the spirituals to the world were disbanded, and black music went underground once more. There was, however, a difference. Blacks were no longer slaves. Although still oppressed and exploited, they did possess a degree of freedom. One of the areas in which this freedom might find expression was in the field of popular entertainment.

As we have already seen, black musicians were an established part of southern plantation life. Throughout the period of slavery, such musicians played a dominant role in the cultural life of the South, entertaining at parties and other social affairs. After emancipation, many of these musicians turned to the theater for their livelihoods. The theater, at the time, meant minstrels.

In this way, black musicians came to take part in a theatrical form that had been dominated by whites who were imitating blacks. This infusion of originals into counterfeits had startling results. Though the black performer was still more or less bound by the long-established stereotypes of minstrelsy, he was able, nevertheless, through details of emphasis and interpretation, to give the songs and dances and instrumental accompaniments an authenticity and an originality that they had not previously possessed. In a very short time, this amalgamation was to produce the first internationally popular American music. It came to be called "ragtime," and it literally swept the world.

In words set to the music of "The Maple Leaf Rag," by Scott Joplin, Sydney Brown said, "I can shake the world's foundation with the Maple Leaf Rag!" He was not very far from wrong. In the two decades before the twentieth century, ragtime music rose rapidly to an immense popularity and became something of a craze. Its syncopated rhythms and sprightly tunes found an enthusiastic audience everywhere. The ragtime mania that gripped the world in the Gay Nineties saw the dancing habits of the world changed overnight. Within a decade the fox trot replaced the waltz as the favorite ballroom dance, and people everywhere were doing the "cakewalk."

As a distinctive, original musical expression, ragtime captured the interest of European composers, who were delighted with the freedom and inventiveness of the form. Claude Debussy, Edward Elgar, Camille Saint-Saëns, and Anton Dvorak were among the eminent composers who utilized the rhythms and spirit of ragtime in their compositions. This interest came when "serious" musicians in America, their musical sensibilities dulled by American racist concepts, had nothing but contempt for this "barbaric" outpouring from the dregs of American society.

Probably the most famous name associated with the rise of ragtime is that of Scott Joplin (1869–1917), born in Texarkana, Texas. As in so many black families, music played a central role in the lives of the Joplins. His mother sang and played the banjo, his father played the violin, and his brother the guitar. All were accomplished musicians whose talents were in constant demand. They played at weddings and at funerals, at celebrations and parties, and became well known in the Texarkana area.

Scott, himself, was attracted to the piano and began learning to play this instrument in a neighbor's house. He was such an enthusiastic pupil that his father managed to save enough money for the purchase of an old-fashioned square grand. A local German musician, impressed by Scott's talent, gave the boy lessons and introduced him to the music of the great European composers, besides teaching him the fundamentals of theory and harmony. For a time, Scott's parents encouraged the boy to become a concert pianist. Scott, however, had ideas of his own.

While still in his teens, he left home to make his way as an itinerant piano player and wandered all over the South and Southwest. This experience brought him into intimate contact with the folklore and the music of other black musicians. In 1885, at the age of 17, Scott came to St. Louis, where he stayed for the next eight years. He played regularly in the honky-tonks and saloons on Chestnut and Market Streets frequented by the black musicians who were developing the free and original style of piano music that was soon to be known as ragtime.

In 1893, Joplin went to Chicago for the World's Columbian Exposition. Here, he met some of the early Chicago ragtime players, such as "Plunk" Henry and John Seymour. It was after he returned to St. Louis that Joplin composed his first songs. These, however, were sentimental ditties, not rags. He wanted to break into the music writing field and did not think that there would be a market for "rags." Joplin, at the time, was still playing ragtime piano in a number of clubs in St. Louis and Sedalia, Missouri. While playing at the Maple Leaf Club in the Summer of 1899, he was heard by John Stillwell Stark, a music publisher. He recognized the originality and vitality of the music immediately and offered to publish Joplin's compositions. The result was the publication, in 1899, of the *Maple Leaf Rag*, with its classic ragtime syncopations over the steady rhythm of the bass.

Maple Leaf Rag was an immediate success. Joplin had signed a royalty contract, so that composer as well as publisher profited from the sales, which were enormous for those times. As a result of this success, Joplin was able to leave the honky-tonks and saloons where he had earned his living. He moved into a large house of his own and set himself up as a piano teacher. He continued composing a succession of rags and other popular pieces. He also wrote a set of etudes for the study of ragtime, *The School of Ragtime: Six Exercises for Piano*, which was published by John Stark in 1908. Joplin, we must remember, was a thoroughly schooled musician who was familiar with the classical literature of the piano. He made no excuses for ragtime and considered it a legitimate as well as important school of music. His book of exercises was directed, not at the beginner, but at the advanced student. In his preface, Joplin wrote:

> What is scurrilously called ragtime is an invention that is here to stay. That is now conceded by all classes of musicians. That all publications masquerading under the name of ragtime are not the genuine article will be better known when these exercises are studied. That real ragtime of the higher class is rather difficult to play is a painful truth which most pianists have discovered. Syncopations are no indication of light or trashy

music, and to shy bricks at "hateful ragtime" no longer passes for musical culture. To assist the amateur players in giving the "Joplin Rags" that weird and intoxicating effect intended by the composer is the object of this work.

Joplin moved to New York City in 1909 where he lived for the rest of his life. Among his compositions are two ragtime operas—*A Guest of Honor,* written in 1903, and *Treemonisha,* 1911. Although neither was successful on the stage, this effort by Scott Joplin marks the first attempt by an American composer to create an American folk opera. In 1917, Joplin's health began to fail. He died on April 1, 1917, famous and honored for the music he had contributed to the world.

Contrary to popular opinion, Irving Berlin's widely performed *Alexander's Ragtime Band,* written in 1911, did not bring in the age of ragtime. Actually, ragtime was already in decline in 1911. Berlin's tune caught the public fancy for a time, but it represented one of the final manifestations of this musical form. What happened to ragtime was to be repeated again and again in American music. Overexploitation by commercial interests, high-pressure promotion of what was no more than pseudo-ragtime at best, the mechanical repetition of routine formulas that soon degenerated into cliché—all contributed to the decline of the form as a vital style of American music.

Ragtime did, however, demonstrate the strong popular appeal of black music. As such, it helped prepare the way for the next wave of music that was to flow out of the black community. Ragtime, said Gilbert Chase in his monumental study *America's Music,* "can be considered as an important tributary of jazz, the Mississippi River of American music."

10 Jazz: The Mississippi River of American Music

Gilbert Chase's metaphor likening jazz to the Mississippi River is doubly appropriate. The Mississippi River is one of the great waterways of the world, and the most important river in America. Running through the heart of the continent, its waters have carried and shaped the history, people, and commerce of this nation. Both the myths and folklore of America testify to its greatness.

However, the Mississippi was also a roadway of music—a rich body of song and dance came into existence and spread along its waterways. For the steamboats that plied the river and its tributaries carried not only cotton and wheat and livestock, they also carried music. It is not surprising that its towns and cities—New Orleans, St. Louis, Memphis, Natchez, Cairo, Sedalia, Minneapolis—came to be centers of American music, where different traditions and styles would come together.

In a similar sense, jazz represents the heart of American music. It is the mainstream of this cultural expression and, together with its musical tributaries, it affects and influences all American music. Today, when learned musicologists discuss the American contribution to the world's musical heritage, all agree upon the significance of this indigenous musical form. Jazz has been the great gift of America to the music of the world.

In its development, jazz is akin to folk music. It grew and flowered on its own, in response to the musical needs of a particular segment of the American population. Jazz, in its initial stages, was the secular music of the American blacks. Initially, commercial considerations had little if any influence on this development.

Like so much of American music, jazz represents a synthesis, a coming-together of various musical traditions and styles. In this sense jazz is a musical hybrid, exhibiting an almost biological hybrid vitality. It drew upon all of the melodic and rhythmic resources of the New World. In jazz we can recognize traces of Baptist hymns and Elizabethan ballads; we hear echoes of black spirituals, of the blues and the old field holler. Jazz rhythms contain hints of the French quadrille along with the syncopated rhythm of ragtime; we can distinguish traces of the foot-tapping pulse of the country hoe-down and mountain reel of Scotch-Irish derivation, along with a memory of a complex and sophisticated African percussive tradition. All of these elements were assimilated and transformed in the formation of that musical flowering we call jazz.

Nor was this a sudden, overnight development. It took some three centuries for the synthesis to be completed. Its history can be traced in the successive waves of music generated by the black experience in America—from African songs and dances to plantation slave music, the minstrel show, ragtime, and blues.

Popular tradition holds that jazz came into existence in the bawdyhouses and saloons of the Storyville section of New Orleans. More accurately, jazz was "in the air" at the turn of the century. Something very much like jazz was being performed at the time wherever black musicians found opportunity to play. "Jelly Roll" Morton, one of the pioneers of jazz, described the situation: "Jazz music is a style, not a composition." It was a style that reflected the musical genius of a people, not a particular city or locale.

Indeed, the entire body of Afro-American music, in all of its varied manifestations, is a single entity, possessed of an organic unity that stems from a common cultural tradition. In its development, this music has borrowed from many sources and taken many paths, but in all of the spirituals and shouts, the work and play songs, the children's songs and lullabies, the cornfield hollers and the blues, the banjo tunes and dances, there is revealed a common ancestry and close kinship, which finds expression in a special "quality" of the music.

Historically, however, the focal point for the development of jazz became New Orleans. There was good reason for this. New Orleans, at the turn of the century, was a tolerant, fun-loving city in whose exuberant life even a black musician might find a place. The annual Mardi Gras, the colorful processions and numerous parades and celebrations that characterized the city, placed a premium on musicians of all kinds.

After the Civil War and emancipation many blacks turned to music as a means of earning their livelihood. Many already were musicians for, as we have already seen, the black musician was a regular feature of plantation life. More important, music provided one of the few areas in which a black man was permitted to excel.

Immediately following the Civil War, bands of newly emancipated street musicians appeared throughout the South. They sang, danced, and performed, generally to the accompaniment of banjo, guitar, and bones, together with the "skat" band—the traditional instruments of the black musician in the South. Many of these street musicians, attracted by the life of the city, made their way to New Orleans, where their musical horizons were broadened.

For one thing, New Orleans had been a center for the manufacture of wind instruments for many years. These were plentiful and inexpensive, especially since a large store of surplus band instruments from both the Confederate and Union armies had come onto the market. Thus, the price of a serviceable instrument came within the range of practically anyone who wanted to make music. Then, the availability of these instruments, together with a large audience for music, led to the organization of bands. No other city in America had so marked a sympathy for band music. In the decades following the Civil War, the sound of the brass band became the hallmark of New Orleans. Bands were everywhere. They were used to advertise sales and to attract people to listen to political speeches. They accompanied funerals, religious and secular processions, patriotic parades, weddings, excursions, and carnivals. Bands from New Orleans entertained on the big Mississippi river boats.

It is a fact that many of these bands were made up of black musicians; a dozen black bands took part in the mammoth funeral cortege for President Garfield in 1881. However, we cannot be certain exactly how these black bands sounded. That is, we do not know to what extent they conformed to conventional standards. We do know, from descriptive accounts of the period, that they did not sound like the usual military marching band. We also know that the black bands were very popular with all the people of New Orleans—a preference that engendered bitter complaints from the white musicians of the time.

For the most part, these black street bands were made up of musicians who worked at other trades and played in their spare time. Most learned to play their instruments without benefit of formal training; they learned through a process of trial and error, through a continual experimentation, and through the application of their own distinctive musical tradition. They played by "ear" rather than "eye." Guided only by their musical intuition and the inspiration of the moment, they transformed popular songs and tunes through the unrestricted play of their intelligence and imagination. In this way, new techniques of performance evolved, full of unorthodox sounds and timbres that were never taught in conventional study. It was a distinct style, characterized by new tonal combinations, never-before-heard dissonances, novel melodic figures, and disjointed counterpoints. In fact, a totally new kind of instrumental tone—since incorporated into the regular techniques of these instruments—was created out of the musicians' imitation of some of the harsh, guttural, throaty sounds that black singers used.

When these instrumental techniques were applied to the syncopated rhythms of ragtime, jazz came into being. Blatant, abandoned, full of driving energy and imagination, often outrageous, inventive, this was a music calculated to shock the sensibilities of genteel America. In New Orleans, it flourished. This was the kind of music that resounded in such notorious pleasure-palaces as *The 101 Ranch, Pete La La's Cafe,* and *The Tuxedo Dance Hall.*

Haunts such as these, along Basin Street in the Storyville section of New Orleans, provided the black musician with opportunities for employment which no other city or district in America could match. It is not surprising that they flocked to this city. Although they were not particularly well paid for their services, and even the best of them had to double at other jobs, they were encouraged and even, at times, idolized. In Storyville, the black musician was afforded the stimulation and acceptance that allowed him the opportunity to develop his highly personal style and technique. In Storyville, the jazz musician was king.

One of the earliest names associated with classic New Orleans jazz is that of Charles "Buddy" Bolden. Tall, slender, strikingly handsome, Bolden was an enterprising citizen of New Orleans—a barber with his own shop and the publisher of a newspaper called *The Cricket.* He learned to play the cornet on his own and organized a band in the early 1890s. Although he never learned how to read music, Bolden exhibited remarkable musical abilities. His inventiveness and style won immediate popularity, and the Bolden band came into wide demand for parades and dances.

For almost 15 years, he was the focal point for New

Orleans music. At one time or another, most of the important jazz pioneers played with Bolden. His reputation assumed such proportions that for years afterward jazz musicians boasted of their association with him. According to Louis Armstrong, Bolden was a "one man genius—way ahead of them all." It was said that on a quiet day the sound of his cornet could be heard for miles. His ability to improvise and embroider a melody with all kinds of exuberant turns and ornaments was an unforgettable aural experience according to those who heard him.

Bolden continued to be a dominant figure in New Orleans jazz right up to the time of his tragic nervous collapse in 1907, while playing in a street parade. Subsequently, he had to be confined to a sanitarium, where he remained till his death in 1931. Although his career was cut short at the height of his powers, Bolden left a significant legacy. He, more than any other figure, gave form to the musical styles and syntax that grew out of the experience of the black ghetto.

After the loss of Bolden, Freddie Keppard (1883–1932) became the central figure in New Orleans jazz. An outstanding cornet player, he organized the Olympia Band in 1909, which reigned as the leading jazz ensemble until the close of Storyville in 1917. Included in Keppard's band—the classic jazz ensemble was rarely larger than seven pieces—were such outstanding musicians as Louis "Big Eye" Nelson (clarinet), Sidney Bechet (clarinet), Willy Santiago (guitar), Zue Robertson (trombone), and King Oliver (cornet).

There were of course, many other bands elsewhere at this time, and they share in the credit for the development of jazz. It was simply that for New Orleans it was a particularly fast-paced, fertile period. Competition between bands as well as individual musicians was intense. Bands played all over the city for practically every public affair. Often, two or more bands, each with its own following of admirers, would cross in the streets. Such an event led to a "cutting match"—a musical free-for-all—in which the bands would try to outdo each other in sheer volume of sound as well as improvisational invention.

These early jazz musicians used whatever songs and melodies were around as springboards for their invention. All music was grist for the jazz mill—patriotic songs, bawdy-house ballads, music hall tunes, spirituals, blues, hymns, French and Spanish dances, minstrel songs. This caldron-like quality of early jazz was described by "Jelly Roll" Morton, in an account of the composition of his own version of "Tiger Rag."

> The Tiger Rag I transformed from an old French quadrille, which was originally in a lot of different tempos. First, there was the introduction—"every body get your partners"—and the people would go rushing around the hall.... The next strain would be a waltz... then another strain which comes right behind the waltz in mazurka time... We had two other strains in two-four time. I transformed these into the *Tiger Rag* which I also named from the way I made the "Tiger" roar with my elbow!... In one of my earliest tunes, *New Orleans Blues*, you can notice the Spanish tinge.... In fact, if you can't put tinges of Spanish into your tunes, you will never be able to get the right seasoning, I call it, for jazz.

However, though the music was often just such a mixture of current styles and songs, the typical orchestration and use of the individual instruments derived directly from the blues. There is an early recording, dating back to 1911 or 1912, of a typical blues song of the period called "When a 'Gator Hollers," sung by Margaret Johnson accompanied by clarinet, cornet, and piano. The instrumentalists are not named, though the cornet player is believed to be King Oliver. In this recording, Margaret Johnson carries the melodic lead, while the two instruments play discreetly under her voice. The piano is used in a percussive sense, providing a steady beat that underlies the performance of the melodic trio. In the "breaks" between voice verses, the cornet comes in with its own strident solos, answering the voice with sighs, sobs, and an occasional chuckle. The clarinet reinforces this effect when the two instruments join, in these bridges, in discordant duets. Singer, clarinet, and cornet thus provide a three-part harmony in a call-and-response pattern reminiscent of the music of West Africa. Replace the singer with the trombone of the jazz era and you still retain the essential form—three voices that sing and answer over an underlying rhythmical base.

Cornet, clarinet, trombone, and trumpet were, in fact, the instruments favored by the early jazzmen as the most flexible and expressive. The trumpet or cornet generally took the "lead" voice, sounding the melodic lines to which the other instruments responded. Clarinet (high voice) and trombone (low voice) completed the three-part harmony. These voices embroidered around the lead melody and took their own melodic breaks in turn. Rhythm came to consist generally of guitar, bass, and drums, while some of the early bands included a banjo and an occasional tuba to round out this section. Later, the piano was incorporated as a dual instrument—the left hand provided a percussive beat while the right hand allowed for another melodic voice.

The New Orleans period of jazz ended in 1913 when all the saloons and dance halls in Storyville were closed because of a brawl in which two men were killed. Deprived of their

livelihood, jazz musicians began to flow from New Orleans
in a mass exodus. By the time Storyville was back in business
again, in late 1914, most of the musicians had already left;
and there were few to mourn its official demise in 1917. From
New Orleans, the musicians streamed north and east to play
in cabarets and honky-tonks in St. Louis and Chicago, Memphis, Cleveland and New York. Most of them were welcomed.
America had had a taste of jazz through the efforts of touring
bands, such as those organized by King Oliver and Freddie
Keppard, and demanded more.

In 1918, King Oliver settled in Chicago where he organized
the influential *Creole Jazz Band*, which included Jimmy
Noone (clarinet), Honore Dutry (trombone), Ed Garland
(bass), Lillian Hardin (piano), and Minor "Ram" Hall
(drums). In 1922, he added a second cornet to the band, a
young player from New Orleans named Louis Armstrong.
This group made a number of recordings in the early twen-
ties which provide the definitive sound of classic New Orleans
jazz. Such tunes as. "Dipper-mouth Blues," "High Society,"
"Canal Street Blues," and "Snake Rag" reveal the rhythmic
and melodic flexibility that was at the heart of the style. The
playing is spontaneous, relaxed, and perfectly controlled,
demonstrating the freedom and inventiveness of this home-
grown musical form.

The Chicago period saw a further development of jazz
style. In its earliest phase the rhythmic base was provided
by the military drum and revolved around a whole-note beat.
During the first decade of the twentieth century, a half-note
beat with syncopation gradually came to be the preferred
meter. Ultimately, this half-note meter was broken up,
occasionally with a tango-like syncopation, until by the late

Louis Armstrong, whose performing career spans three generations, was a pivotal figure in the development of American jazz. *(United Press International Photo)*

Fletcher Henderson (right) with Benny Goodman, was one of the innovators of "big band swing" which dominated American popular music from the 1930s to the 1950s. *(Wide World)*

Duke Ellington's compositions and performances helped elevate jazz to the level of "fine art" music. *(United Press International Photo)*

Charlie Parker (right) on alto sax, with "Hot Lips" Page, on trumpet, was an important influence on the development of modern, improvisational jazz. (*United Press International Photo*)

Charlie Mingus, bassist and composer, is a dominant figure in today's "progressive" jazz. (*United Press International Photo*)

Aretha Franklin, with roots in gospel singing, extends a musical tradition that came to America from Africa—a tradition that continues to play a dominant role in American music. (*Atlantic Records*)

1920s Louis Armstrong had made a quarter-note rhythm irrevocable.

The next important phase in the history of jazz takes us to New York City. In 1919, a black pianist from Georgia, named Fletcher Henderson, organized a radically different kind of jazz band, which played at the Roseland dance hall. Henderson's band was big, much bigger than the usual jazz ensemble, featuring as many as 25 musicians. The sheer size of the band made improvisation, which had been at the heart of jazz till this time, awkward, if not impossible. Groups of more than 9 players cannot achieve the spontaneous cohesion and the smooth ensemble necessary for an improvisational jazz performance. Thus, in Henderson's band, the musicians did not improvise. Instead, Henderson prepared orchestral arrangements, written out in advance and carefully rehearsed before the performance. What Henderson's band lost in spontaneity was made up in sonority and the rich musical effects that could be generated by a large number of instruments playing together.

More important, Henderson's big band was commercially successful. The public responded to the rich sounds and driving rhythms generated by this kind of ensemble. Roseland became a center for this new type of jazz, and the crowds that were drawn to this New York dance hall inspired an avalanche of imitators. The Henderson band played in Roseland for almost 15 years and included in its roster some of the finest jazz musicians of the time, including Louis Armstrong and Coleman Hawkins.

Another important influence on this type of big-band jazz was Edward "Duke" Ellington. Born in Washington, D.C., in 1899, Ellington studied music at the Pratt Institute and formed his first band, a small one, in 1918. Although this band followed the popular New Orleans style of the period, Ellington had definite ideas about the direction jazz was going to take. From the beginning, he tried to create a personal style, an individual expression in the tradition of the art composer. His compositions are characterized by sophistication, rhythmic smoothness, and originality and include what many musicologists consider masterpieces of jazz-inspired orchestral compositions. Ellington quicky rose to national and international fame, touring Europe with immense success in 1933.

The ideas of Henderson and Ellington pointed the way. By the beginning of the 1930s the big band dominated jazz. What happened was that the large dance bands were commercially successful while the small "hot" groups were not. The situation came to a peak in the overblown, slick ensembles exploited by Paul Whiteman and other musical impresarios in the mid-1930s. This new sound was called "swing," and it swept the nation.

In the face of this slick competition, jazz in the New Orleans tradition of spontaneous improvisation practically disappeared. Eddie Condon, the noted jazz guitarist, summed up the situation: "Just about the only place we could play was in our own rooms, at our own request." Jazz was confronting a crisis similar to that which led to the demise of ragtime. Having come into the hands of commercial interests, it was being overexposed and overpromoted, while the music itself was losing its distinctive character.

A generation of musicians grew up in the 1930s chafing at the bit imposed by the big-band concept of swing. Brilliant and beautiful and slick as the big band was, it was also completely removed from the original feeling of jazz. The inspired performer was lost in the sections of the big band and had to settle for informal "jam" sessions, held in the privacy of the dressing room between shows, to create any kind of personal expression. With this in mind, we can appreciate the instrumental revolt against the big-band, which was in full swing by the mid-1940s. It was spearheaded by black musicians, almost exclusively. The result was a return to the improvisational tradition of early New Orleans jazz—with one big difference. The musicians who instituted the revolt were more capable, in every aspect of musicianship and instrumental competence, than their untutored predecessors. All were musically literate, with a theoretical background in music and a solid instrumental foundation—the new professional requirements of the trade.

The results were brilliant. Powered by musicians of the caliber of Charlie Parker, Thelonius Monk, Dizzy Gillespie, and Miles Davis, the music exploded into an astonishing glissando of abstract sound, a development that marked an important turning point in the growth of jazz.

Until this time jazz was primarily a popular folk music form. It was performed to be danced to, and its basic function was to involve the listener in active physical participation. As such its musical development was restricted by the demands of the dance floor. Now, during the 1940s, jazz—improvisational jazz performed by small, intimate groups—was liberated from the dance floor. It became music for listening, an art form. The inventive brilliance of Charlie Parker was a prime moving force in this direction. Parker had original ideas about the functions of rhythm, melody, and phrase length and a sweeping harmonic and melodic imagination.

As a result of Parker's influence, the rhythm section came

to provide a new function in the jazz ensemble. It gave up the steady metronomic pulse and took the drummer's foot off the bass pedal, allowing the rhythm section the freedom necessary to accent the new rhythms that the soloists were generating in their new improvisational flights. The new sound was called "bop"—after a rhythmic figure—and it found an enthusiastic new audience.

This new jazz language was formalized and further refined in the 1950s. Jazz became "cool," as epitomized in a group of orchestral recordings made by trumpeter Miles Davis with a medium-sized group. This phase was marked by further rhythmic freedom and a sophisticated harmonic development. One of the members of Davis's group was John Lewis, who later organized the Modern Jazz Quartet, a jazz-improvisation group that adapted aspects of classic counterpoint and harmonic development.

Another pioneer during this period was Thelonius Monk, whose compositions for small groups, such as *Four In One* and *Criss-Cross*, introduced the idea of thematically—rather than harmonically—developed improvisation, as a form within the jazz tradition. Exploiting this basic idea, tenor saxophonist Theodore "Sonny" Rollins became one of the first horn players in jazz to perform an extended improvisation with thematic development and cohesion.

Ornette Coleman has probably carried the "cool" style of jazz to its furthest extreme to date. Coleman's most important innovations are rhythmic and have introduced a concept that is almost African in its subtlety to group playing. In Coleman's groups drummer and bass may play entirely different rhythmic patterns, simultaneously, against a rhythm generated out of the flights of the solo instruments through the phrasing of improvised melodic lines.

Intonation in the Coleman style is also free, with the traditional "blue" notes and vocal inflections elevated to a point where they encompass entire melodic phrases and lines. Improvisation in the Coleman style is based on a general thematic outline rather than on the harmonic progression of a theme melody. This style represents a triumph of improvisation over all other aspects of musical structure.

Here, then, was a brief history of jazz. It is one of the most exciting chapters in all of music. What began as a "bottom-waving, vulgar, barbaric howl" has been transformed into a sophisticated, even esoteric, lady. Jazz has moved from the saloon to the concert hall, and, in so doing, has brought back improvisation, which had all but disappeared after the baroque period.

This development has taken place within the short span of 50 years. During this time, jazz has exerted a continuous influence on all aspects of American music. Its beat, its swing, its earthiness have provided the base upon which the whole edifice of popular music has been constructed. Although jazz today hardly qualifies as "popular" music— it is too highly developed and sophisticated to be placed in this category—it has left its mark and its sound on the music of the world.

11 Today

Throughout the twentieth century the music that has flowed from the black community has been the dominant influence in American music. This, of course, does not mean that only black musicians have been involved in this development. White musicians and composers from many different ethnic backgrounds have also played a role. Still, the kinds of songs we sing, the dances we dance to, the use of the instruments in our bands and orchestras, the distinctive quality of American music can be traced, even if indirectly, to the musical genius that came to the New World from Africa.

The most recent example of this influence has been the rock and roll revolution, which continues to dominate popular musical expression in America as this is being written. Here, as if to demonstrate its continuing vitality, black America has provided still another musical wave that has found its way into the mainstream of American music.

The factors that went into the creation of this great musical shout of the 1960s are many and complex. It would be all but impossible to define them with any degree of completeness. We can, however, trace the broad outlines of this development and get some idea of its history. We can start with the change that took place in jazz during the latter part of the 1930s, when it was absorbed into the big-band sound and lost its spontaneous spirit. These huge bands, as we have seen, took the jazz of improvisation and forced it into the rolling beat of swing. Spontaneity and individual invention were subordinated to the sonorous richness of the heavy orchestration. The music of the big band advanced steadily along tracks that were as carefully planned and arranged as those of a railroad. The sound was lush and polished, leaning heavily on brass and massed saxophones.

But brilliant, slick, and beautiful as the big band undoubtedly was, its music began to grow arid once it lost its creative heart, which was rooted in jazz. Swing, as generated by the big bands, was completely opposed to the spontaneous, improvisational spirit of jazz. There was no place for free individual expression in its complex and sophisticated arrangements.

True jazz, meanwhile, had taken a different turn. After World War II, many jazz musicians felt the need to return to the small intimate ensemble and the old New Orleans tradition of improvisation. Here, however, all resemblance ended. Originally, jazz had been the music for a vigorous and earthy dance style. It was performed by musicians of genius who, nevertheless, were musically illiterate.

The new jazz, championed by musicians who shared in the musical genius of their predecessors but also brought musical sophistication to their art, took the classic improvisational style down unexpected bypaths. Jazz became something else. Ignoring the traditional association with dance, these new performers burst into abstract patterns of sound. In a way, they cut down to the heart of jazz; but, at the same time, they did something strange and new. Their music was for listening only. It became "cool" and reflected a kind of Bauhaus purity of expression.

Then, as the progressive jazzmen dipped still deeper in their explorations of the improvisational art, their music became even more abstract and pure. Finally, it resembled nothing so much as a sound version of what the abstract expressionist painters were creating on canvas. The dance was completely forsaken in the interest of sound.

The big band, meanwhile, found itself in a creative crisis during the 1940s and early 1950s. Having divorced itself from the earthy forms of jazz, its sound was degenerating into a vapid manipulation of cliché. Popular music during this brief period was coming from three areas: Broadway shows, Hollywood musicals, and the novelty factories of Tin Pan Alley. It was a bleak period for popular music.

At the same time, however, another kind of music was developing in the hinterlands; in fact, there were a number of nascent musical styles, examples of which would surface now and again. There was rhythm and blues—a music that was, for the most part, limited to the black community; there was gospel—black church music sung with powerful rhythm and equally powerful emotional drive; and there was country and western, a style sneered at as "hillbilly" by knowing city folk.

It was out of a synthesis of these different kinds of music that the earthy, vital sound of today was to evolve. The process was slow and gradual. Jazz, as we have seen, became big-band on the one hand, and esoteric on the other. But, in both cases, it lost its root appeal. Then, rhythm and blues burst on the scene; and when it had absorbed gospel and country and western, it became rock and roll and outranked everything else.

First, it was deep South, or country, blues, with a heady admixture of the massive rhythms of gospel. Then came the electric guitars, the high, amplified sound with a generous dose of country and western. In the late 1940s and early 1950s, such germinal black performers as Chuck Berry, Bo Diddley, Muddy Waters, and John Lee Hooker were creating a music that was gaining vociferous admirers. Their recordings began to appear on the charts as best-sellers.

In the industry, most of these records were referred to as "race" records. That is, they were made primarily by and for blacks. They were, however, played on the radio—featured by black disc jockeys on black programs—and anyone could tune in a radio station. It soon became evident that droves of teenagers—black and white—were turning to the "race" stations.

That was the beginning. The new sound, originating in the "race" stations, caught on and spread. Soon, enterprising white disc jockeys began to exploit this "rich vein of music" that was emanating from the black community. The first important breakthrough came in 1954, when a number of songs performed by a group called *The Crows* rocketed to the top of the charts. The Crows sang a pure strain of rhythm and blues in the three hit records—"Hucklebuck," "Long Gone," and "Pink Champagne."

The rest is history. Rock and roll spread in a wave that engulfed the world. This gift of black America reached into England, where it ignited a musical explosion whose brightness has dazzled the world. Overnight, it changed the dancing patterns of generations, releasing the stiffness of joints immobilized for centuries. Eldridge Cleaver, in his book *Soul On Ice*, described this phenomenon like this:

> The Twist...burst upon the scene like a nuclear explosion, sending its fallout of rhythm into the Minds and Bodies of the people. The fallout: the Hully Gully, the Mashed Potato, the Dog, the Smashed Banana, the Watusi, the Frug, the Swim. The Twist was a guided missile, launched from the ghetto into the very heart of suburbia. The Twist succeeded, as politics, religion, and law could never do, in writing in the heart and soul what the Supreme Court could only write in a book.

Today, we can hear this echo of Africa, which welled up through the bloody experience of American blacks, all over the world. In Japan, a thriving cult of Americana has evolved around the rhythms of this sound. In Russia, bootlegged Jimmy Hendrix recordings, taped from Voice of America broadcasts, command a premium price on the black market and are passed lovingly from hand to hand as rare cultural treasures. In Italian night clubs, go-go girls are doing the frug. England's principal export, or so it might seem, has become music—music derived from this fountainhead.

How do we explain this universal acceptance? Why should a boy from the slums of Liverpool turn on to a music that came to life in the black slave warrens of South Carolina?

Why should a youth in Sicily place his hard-earned coins into a machine to hear the sound of a Ray Charles in the soft, lemon-scented Sicilian night? Why should a young man in Japan, with a cultural background so foreign, so different, pick up a guitar and sing "the blues"?

It is not a question of promotion and clever exploitation. It goes far deeper than this. There is a quality in this music that enables it to span oceans, to bridge the deepest cultural chasms, and focus upon a common humanity that all God's children share. It is this terribly human quality that characterizes black music, this humanity which strikes a responsive chord in all. Eldridge Cleaver, again, said it like this:

> It is with his music and dance, the recreation through art of the rhythms suggested by and implicit in the tempo of his life and cultural environment, that man purges his soul of the tensions of daily strife and maintains his harmony in the universe.... Into this music, the Negro projected—as it were, *drained off*, as pus from a sore—a powerful sensuality, his pain and lust, his love and his hate, his ambition and his despair. The Negro projected into his music his very Body.

This is a music that has been some 400 years in the making. A music that was once a question of life and death—nothing less. To understand this, we must go back to the black slaves who brought this music from Africa. For everyone that reached America alive, five died either on the forced marches to the sea in Africa or on shipboard in the infamous "middle passage." The survivors who reached these shores were as close to being dead as any forcibly transported people in history.

All this dying was bad for business. A live slave was a negotiable asset; a dead one was worthless. The slave traders, being practical men, tried to reduce this disastrous

mortality rate. They gave the slaves good red beans to eat
and clean water to drink. Sometimes they gave them better
quarters than those of the crew, but still the cargo insisted
on dying.

Then someone discovered that if you made the slaves sing
and dance they stayed alive. Just plain exercise was no good.
It had to be the charleston, the lindy, and the twist—more
accurately, the African originals of these dances. It was this
consideration, in 1700, that led Thomas Starks, a London
merchant in the slave trade, to write the captain of the bark
Africa, which had taken on a cargo of 450 slaves from the
Gold Coast: "Make your Negroes cheerful and pleasant, making them dance to the beating of the drum...."

It is this music, modified and altered through countless
evolutions, to which we listen and respond. It gave birth
to the spiritual and the blues, to ragtime and jazz, to gospel
song and rock and roll. It represents the single most significant cultural contribution made by any minority group to
America.

Still, neither the history of this people nor its music is
complete. Both are still very much with us, more so perhaps
today than ever before. And both this history and music
have a message for America that must be heeded—a message that was eloquently spelled out by W. E. B. Du Bois:

Your country? How came it yours? Before the Pilgrims landed
we were here. Here we have brought our three gifts and
mingled them with yours: a gift of story and song—soft, stirring
melody in an ill-harmonized and unmelodious land; the gift of
sweat and brawn to beat back the wilderness, conquer the soil,
and lay the foundations of this vast economic empire two
hundred years earlier than your weak hands could have done
it; the third, a gift of the Spirit. Around us the history of the

land has centered for thrice a hundred years; out of the nation's heart we have called all that was best to throttle and subdue all that was worst; fire and blood, prayer and sacrifice, have billowed over this people, and they have found peace only in the altars of the God of Right. Nor has our gift of the spirit been merely passive. Actively we have woven ourselves with the very warp and woof of this nation,—we fought their battles, shared their sorrow, mingled our blood with theirs, and generation after generation have pleaded with a headstrong, careless people to despise not Justice, Mercy and Truth, lest the nation be smitten with a curse. Our song, our toil, our cheer, and warning have been given to the nation in blood-brotherhood. Are not these gifts worth the giving? Is not this work and striving? Would America have been America without her Negro people?

Bibliography

Aptheker, Herbert, ed. *A Documentary History of the Negro People in the United States*. New York: Citadel Press, 1951.

_____. *The Negro in the Civil War*. New York: International Publishers, 1938.

_____. *The Negro in the American Revolution*. New York: International Publishers, 1940.

Armstrong, Louis. *Swing That Music*. London: Longmans, Green and Co., 1936.

Bancroft, Frederic. *Slave-Trading in the Old South*. Baltimore: J. H. Furst Company, 1931.

Bennet, Lerone, Jr. *Before the Mayflower*. Chicago: Johnson Publishing Co., 1962.

Blesh, Rudi and Harriet Janis. *They All Played Ragtime*. New York: Alfred Knopf, 1950.

Bohannan, Paul. *Africa and Africans*. New York: Natural History Press, 1964.

Boulton, Laura. *The Music Hunter*. New York: Doubleday, 1969.

Chase, Gilbert. *America's Music*. New York: McGraw-Hill, 1955.

Cleaver, Eldridge. *Soul On Ice*. New York: Dell Publishing Co., 1968.

Courlander, Harold. *Negro Folk Music U.S.A.* New York: Columbia University Press, 1963.

Du Bois, William E. B. *Black Folk: Then and Now*. New York: H. Holt and Co., 1939.

_____. *The Souls of Black Folk*. Chicago: A. C. McGlurge and Co., 1903.

Elkins, Stanley M. *Slavery, A Problem in American Institutional and Intellectual Life*. Chicago: University of Chicago Press, 1959.

Finkelstein, Sidney. *Jazz: A People's Music*. New York: Citadel Press, 1948.

Gaines, Francis P. *The Southern Plantation*. Gloucester, Mass.: P. Smith Press, 1962.

Handy, W. C. *Father of the Blues: An Autobiography*. New York: Macmillan, 1940.

Hare, Maud. *Negro Musicians and Their Music*. Washington, D. C.: The Associated Publishers, Inc., 1936.

Herskovits, Melville J. *The Myth of the Negro's Past*. New York: Harper and Bros., 1941.

Higginson, Thomas W. *Army Life in a Black Regiment*. Boston: Beacon Press, 1870; reprinted, 1962.

Howard, John Tasker. *Our American Music*. New York: T. Y. Crowell Co., 1946.

Joplin, Scott. *The School of Ragtime: Six Exercises for the Piano*. St. Louis: J. Stark Publishing Co., 1908.

Krehbiel, H. E. *Afro-American Folksongs*. New York: G. Schirmer, 1913.

Odum, H. W. *Social and Mental Traits of the American Negro*. New York: Columbia University Press, 1910.

Phillips, Ulrich B. *Life and Labor in the Old South*. Boston: Little, Brown and Co., 1929.

Rice, Edward L. *Monarchs of Minstrelsy*. New York: Kenny Publishing Co., 1911.

Spaeth, Sigmund. *A History of Popular Music in America*. New York: Random House, 1948.

Stampp, Kenneth M. *The Peculiar Institution*. New York: Alfred Knopf, 1956.

Vlahos, Olivia. *African Beginnings*. New York: Viking Press, 1967.

Waterman, Richard A. *African Influences on the Music of America*. International Congress of Americanists, Vol. 2, Chicago, 1952.

Williams, Eric. *Capitalism and Slavery*. New York: Russell & Russell, 1961.

Index

145